An Introduction to the
TRADITIONAL COSTUMES
of SABAH

AN INTRODUCTION TO THE TRADITIONAL COSTUMES *of* SABAH

edited by
Rita Lasimbang and Stella Moo-Tan

Contributors
Patricia Regis, Madelon Boeye, Joseph Guntavid, Sintiong Gelet, Su Chin Sidih, Anthony Chong, Kamin Sidek, Judeth John-Baptist, Joseph Tadem, and Nismah Kanak

Ink illustrations by
Dominic Linggu, Yong Ket Hyun, Tay Kian Hiong, and Yap Yun Hun

Natural History Publications
Kota Kinabalu

in association with

Department of Sabah Museum
Kota Kinabalu

1997

Published by

Natural History Publications (Borneo) Sdn. Bhd.
A913, 9th Floor, Wisma Merdeka,
P.O. Box 13908,
88846 Kota Kinabalu, Sabah, Malaysia.
Tel: 088-233098 Fax: 088-240768

in association with

Department of Sabah Museum,
Jalan Muzium,
88300 Kota Kinabalu, Sabah, Malaysia.

First published 1997

Co-editors: Rita Lasimbang
Stella Moo-Tan

Perpustakaan Negara Malaysia Cataloguing-in-Publication Data

An introduction to the traditional costumes of Sabah / edited by
Rita Lasimbang and Stella Moo-Tan.
Bibliography: p. 104
includes index
ISBN 983-812-013-8
1. Costumes—Sabah. 2. Ethnology—Sabah—Social Life and customs. 3. Indigenous peoples—Sabah—Social Life and customs.
I. Rita Lasimbang. II. Moo-Tan, Stella.
391.00959521

Layout and design by C.L. Chan and Chua Kok Hian

Printed in Malaysia.

CONTENTS

Foreword

It is a privilege for the Sabah Museum to co-publish with Natural History Publications Sdn. Bhd. this book on the traditional costumes and attires of seven of Sabah's indigenous groups. Sabah's indigenous population is made up of some 50 groups, and therefore one can see that much still has to be done in documenting all of their costume heritage. This book is but a beginning in the accurate documentation of a colourful aspect of the State's diverse culture.

We are very thankful to Natural History Publications Sdn. Bhd. for their role in the production of this book. I would also like to commend the editors for an excellent job in compiling the research information into a publishable form. Without their perseverence, such a daunting task would not have been accomplished. They have patiently and painstakingly gone through the text numerous times, and I believe they have worked well together in editing this book. As the book goes into print, one of the co-editors, Ms. Rita Lasimbang is no longer in our employ since December 1995. She has however, continued to work on the book despite her new commitments. Though rather delayed, the publication of this book is a reward for the editors' hard work and for all those who have contributed to make it a success.

Mohd. Yunus Hj. Awang Hashim,
The Director,
Sabah Museum,
Kota Kinabalu

Preface

In any society, what people wear or do not wear provides the most basic description of a people. Clothing serves to fulfill a fundamental human need. But how it is worn often demonstrates the identity of the people or group. However, how it covers, protects and distinguishes the person from others is governed by a number of inter-related factors, the most important of which are the physical environment and culture. The climate will dictate the type of clothing to be worn. The plants and animals in the vicinity will determine the raw materials with which to make the clothes. Culture and skills—innate, learned or borrowed—will ascertain the quality, aesthetics and the presentation. The inter-play of these factors will establish the final product—the costume. In Sabah in general, costumes are not static entities. Many are in a state of change. As certain skills become diminished, as new time-saving technologies are adopted, as new commercial products become easily available, the handcrafted costume becomes an artefact of the past. Many have been virtually transformed. Nevertheless, costume production is flourishing in Sabah. The demands of the tourist trade, the development of the performing arts and last but not least, the cultural sentiments of the people have ensured their continuation.

This book is by no means a definitive piece of work on the costumes of Sabah. It is largely about the costumes in the Sabah Museum, and which by definition, are artefacts of the past. The subject is very wide, and much of the information about local costumes, written or oral, remain obscure and fragmentary. The many gaps in both the historical and ethnographic records have therefore limited the number of costumes in this publication to seven, representing seven different indigenous communities. Sabah has some 50 ethnic groups but not all of them wear costumes distinguishable from one another. In fact, many wear similar, if not the same, costumes. Still, the range of indigenous costumes that various people wear in Sabah is wide and varied. Many are worthy of attention, but have not been described in this book for lack of information.

Therefore, the material presented in this book should be regarded only as an introduction to a prominent and visible aspect of Sabah's cultural heritage. The book was also conceived out of a need to serve two purposes. One was to complement the Sabah Museum's permanent exhibition of costumes and textiles entitled "Colours, Cloth and Cosmos" which was opened to the public in May 1994. The other was to meet the mounting demand for information relating to Sabah's people and their traditions. At the same time, it is designed to encourage readers and users of this book to come forward and help the Sabah Museum document the costume heritage.

Comparatively very little has been written about Sabah's people and their cultural traditions. In fact, very few ethnographic studies have been conducted at all. This is due in part, to the absence of a coherent research policy for such studies to take place. Rapid social and physical changes are also occurring before adequate research and documentation can be carried out, aggravated by the lack of trained personnel and appropriate funding. In recent years increasing demand for ethnographic information from various quarters has only highlighted these deficiencies. A large part of this demand has come from various communities who are seeking to establish and promote their identity and culture for nationalistic and cultural sentiments. Tourism has largely contributed to this development. However, it has been discovered that the information gathered in haste to serve the tourist industry has not always been satisfactory. Insufficient data has created inaccuracies. Unfortunately, published material containing these errors tend to perpetuate them. If uncorrected, such information may, over time be regarded as facts. The need for published authoritative studies has become urgent. This book which is by no means comprehensive, is therefore also an attempt to straighten some of the published records.

The Sabah Museum, over the years, has been collecting costumes and gathering associated information as part of its preservation function. But the task of obtaining accurate and consistent information from both published sources and from informants through interviews has been difficult. Many requests for information on costumes and related information have been sent out to district offices, cultural associations and through the Sabah Museum network of informants, but the response has not always been satisfactory. As costumes constitute an important part of Sabah's living heritage, the deficiencies had to be overcome in some way. Thus, a project was initiated three years ago to systematically collect and record costumes for display. The research conducted by Sabah Museum staff was co-ordinated by Ms Madelon Boeye, a free-lance Dutch art historian, who spent three months (in 1993) at the Sabah Museum, training staff, gathering material and planning the costume and textile exhibition. Her work, supported by a small grant from the Royal Netherlands Government, included research in Dutch archives in the Netherlands and translating old Dutch articles on North Borneo into English. In her research, she discovered a number of discrepancies in the existing published material. These have remained on the record, uncorrected. To present an accurate but simple account therefore, became the guiding principle of this book. The labelled illustrations with the minimum of text are designed to serve as a convenient reference for the user. Although only the more outstanding costumes of seven indigenous communities are presented in this book, it is a start for others to be researched and published in the same way.

Much more information is required about the other costumes worn by the people in Sabah. But how much else is published or displayed depends largely on the goodwill and integrity of the public to support the Sabah Museum's aims and objectives.

Patricia Regis

Photo: C.L. Chan

A young Kadazan girl from Kampung Kibabaig, Penampang in her traditional costume.

INTRODUCTION

Sabah, Malaysia's second largest and easternmost state, occupies the northern portion of the Island of Borneo. Her shores are washed on three sides by the South China Sea on the west, the Sulu Sea on the north-east and the Celebes Sea on the south-east, while in the south she shares a common land border with Sarawak and Kalimantan. Located just below the typhoon belt, Sabah has an equable tropical climate which has earned for her the name "Land Below the Wind" from sea-farers who for centuries sought shelter in her long indented coastline during those seasonal destructive storms. She resumed her old name, Sabah, in 1963, at independence. For nearly 80 years under British rule by the British North Borneo Chartered Company (1881–1941), and as a British Crown Colony (1945–1963), Sabah had been known as North Borneo.

Throughout the ages, just like the rest of the South-east Asian archipelago, Borneo has been affected by powerful external, continental influences from mainland Asia. In pre-historic times, between the fifth and second century B.C., aspects of the Dong-son culture, which had its base in Vietnam, had spread over the islands. However, because of its insular isolation, the northern extreme and the interior of Borneo was largely bypassed by other great and colourful traditions, be they religious or cultural. The Hindu and Buddhist empires which arose and extended their influence over much of South-east Asia were unable to penetrate Borneo's dense forest and rugged terrain. Neither did the refined cultures of the Indian sub-continent with their intricate and colourful weaving traditions which left their mark on local material culture elsewhere in the region reached the state. Although carnelian beads, which are objects of great value and still sought after by many ethnic groups, seem to have been imported from India at a very early age.

Hostile tribes also discouraged foreign colonisation and habitation of the interior. Only the coasts and accessible rivers allowed immigrant settlements, formed largely by sea-faring communities. Chinese trade also left traces. A Chinese province was established on the Kinabatangan River in the 14th century, initially to trade and which later developed political marriage alliances with local rulers.

Of the external influences, Islam had the greatest impact. It appeared around the 15th century, brought in by Muslim traders who visited the neighbouring Philippines and left a lasting impression on local culture and customs, especially those of coastal communities, who have remained predominantly Muslim till today. These people and other indigenous inhabitants of the hinterland have also a long history of unrestricted movement across borders, often indifferent to the political boundaries that divide them. As a result, many ethnic groups were created through marriage, migration and other demographic factors. Ethnic labels were often arbitrary, a phenomenon that continues to baffle the authorities even to this day. By the time the Europeans arrived in the 19th century, Sabah was already inhabited by a profusion of peoples and cultures which defied simple ethnic classification.

Sabah's population is heterogenous and culturally diverse, comprising some 50 ethnic groups, of whom about 30 are indigenous to the state. Languages are equally numerous and complex. The languages spoken by Sabah's indigenous peoples belong to the Austronesian language family. As more information about local languages and cultures become available, certain characteristics about these groups have emerged to allow a general ethnic classification. They can be broadly classified according to three categories of people.

The largest category are the Dusun/Kadazan, a collection of tribes who are predominantly wet rice and hill rice cultivators, living on the northern and western coastal plains. Their languages belong to the Dusunic language family. Aside from language, they also share a common animistic belief system with variations in customs and practice. Each tribe may be distinguished from one another by their material culture, the most salient of which is their attire.

An important but smaller group of tribes are the Murut and related sub-groups who live in the far reaches of the interior and in the southern region bordering Kalimantan and Sarawak. Until recently they were a remote and isolated group of people observing a nomadic lifestyle. The

Murut are traditionally subsistence farmers, still practising swidden agriculture, and are known particularly for their hunting skills.

The third category comprise the sea-faring peoples who are predominantly Muslim. These are the Bajaus and their kindred groups, many of whom have lived for hundreds of years on the coasts. They have been joined recently by other immigrant groups from the Philippines and Indonesia, and collectively they have often been described as Malays, a general classification which is somewhat misleading, since these groups display great variations in their culture, languages and customs. These people also show a taste for bright multi-colours in their dress and furnishings, and also for elaborate floral motifs in their other crafts, an element which appear to have been greatly inspired by Islam. The use of colours and such artefacts, however, has not been exclusive to these groups. Over the years a great deal of objects, ideas and concepts have been traded or exchanged between the Bajau and other groups living in the vicinity, arising from their symbiotic relationships. This is evident from the objects and dress of the Dusun/Kadazan who live near them.

The Chinese constitute an important category of people, being the largest non-Austronesian and non-indigenous group in Sabah. They came in large numbers towards the end of the 19th century and at the turn of this century. Many have settled here and intermarried with local indigenous people. In subtle ways they have introduced material, motifs and other ingredients of Chinese culture that have been adopted by native peoples and incorporated into the indigenous material culture.

One of the most definitive statements about a people and their identity is their traditional attire. Costumes are the most prominent visual expression of an ethnic group. In the need to establish their cultural identity and distinguish themselves from other groups, indigenous people have developed and created dress forms and styles which seldom resemble the original artefact. At the same time, in the bid to outshine others, they have also produced the most colourful and eye-catching costume that is probably far more suitable for the stage. Fundamentally, this is due to the fact that dancing costumes have been frequently taken as a symbol of a community's identity. The demands of the tourist industry has largely promoted this development. The borrowing of styles from other groups, modification, adaptation, and of late, the extensive use of glittering and shiny material by some groups to embellish their otherwise traditionally plain attire, have resulted in costumes that over time begin to look similar and familiar. To the purist, this development seems to be a travesty of tradition. However, many indigenous people wear these modified and adapted forms and accept them as traditional. In fact, most of the traditional costumes worn by Sabah's indigenous people are really modern adaptations of the original attire.

The evolution of these modern "traditional" costumes also reflect the social and physical changes that are occurring in the environment. The scarcity of certain raw materials to produce handmade costumes has led to the extensive use of commercial substitutes. Coupled with this, traditional skills are also gradually diminishing as young people prefer to adopt less time consuming methods of production. Among those groups, such as the Lotud of Tuaran, who maintain their traditional costume, styles and form, imported cloth has replaced hand-woven fabric. Others have exchanged homespun yarn processed from homegrown or raw fibre gathered from the wilds in the local environment for commercial, natural and synthetic fibres. Generally, the old and new adapted pieces may look similar in appearance, but on closer inspection, the quality of the handwork on the older pieces are usually finer and superior. This is evident in the traditional embroidery of the older Dusun/Kadazan women who prefer fine and unobtrusive needlework which is a distinguishable feature of their group.

To maintain the traditional forms, people also imitate styles and motifs. One of these is the *linangkit*, which is probably a copy of the weaving technique called *rangkit,* woven on the backstrap loom used by certain Muslim groups in Southern Philippines. Instead of a loom, the *linangkit* is created by using needle and thread to form a dense fabric of interlacing knots. Both *rangkit* and *linangkit* which are strips of fabric, are used by the various tribes in the two countries to decorate and join the seams of their *sarong* or skirt. The Kadazan of Papar also imitate the use of these decorative panels by employing the more simple method of cross-stitch embroidery.

One of the most profound changes to the development of local costumes has been brought about by the introduction of the great monotheistic religions of Islam and Christianity. Improved transportation and communications, such as television information and other influences of the outside world, have reached even the most distant village of the interior. Values and subsequently culture have gradually changed. Consequently, the costumes of certain tribes have become virtually transformed. The notions of modesty that came with these religions resulted in the covering of previously exposed parts of the body. As recently as 20 years ago, it was not uncommon to see the men of certain tribes deep in the interior wearing only loincloths, and their women only skirts. The progressive covering of the body also discouraged another traditional form of decoration and beautification—tattooing—which also used to be an indicator of social status. With the current interest in presenting authenticity, Murut men have returned to the use of bark cloth jackets and loincloths, albeit, enhanced with modern trimmings, to wear only on special occasions to represent their group. Their women have retained their modified black outfits of heavily beaded long skirt and blouse, which they now regard as representative of their identity. The transformation of the Murut costume, thus presents a useful index of some fundamental changes that are taking place in their society.

An interesting feature of Sabah's costume and textile tradition is the relative lack of social status and value of textiles in Sabah. This may be due to the largely egalitarian character of most of its communities. The hierarchy of the social pyramid of the more or less nomadic communities and even those of the more sedentary groups in Sabah has always been low. This makes it unnecessary for one class of people to distinguish itself from another by wearing more elaborate and sophisticated costumes. Exceptions to these are those worn during special events such as weddings and those donned by ritual specialists during religious performances and which differentiate the wearers from the common folk on these occasions.

The sophisticated textiles of mainland Asia, Indonesia, and the intricate warp *ikat* of the indigenous people in other parts of Borneo are conspicuously absent in the north of the island. However, strong cultural influences from the southern Philippines can be detected in the Sabah indigenous costumes and textiles. Many items on both sides of the border are similar. In fact, many accessories have been, and still are, imported from the Philippines. The similarities and common usage of certain cultural objects have their origins in the relatively free movement of peoples over the centuries between the two countries.

The complicated vegetable dyeing methods also require some sedentary residence, and time to learn and to carry out the process. Not all the ingredients may be available in the vicinity. What is lacking may have to be acquired from further afield, through trade or barter. Sabah's indigenous people, other than those on the coasts, generally favour the predominantly black colour combination with red decoration on the costumes. The other basic 'colours' are the undyed natural hues of local fibres and materials. The black or deep-blue dye is usually extracted from indigo (*Indigofera cf. tinctoria*), and the red is obtained from liquid concoctions of the root of *mengkudu* (*Morinda citrifolia*) or solutions of wood shavings of *sapang* (*Caesalpinia sappan*). In recent years, gold and silver accessories and trimmings have been added to brighten the usually plain coloured cloth. Unfortunately, the shiny embellishments are often unaesthetic, neither improving the beauty nor enhancing the simple lines of the original artefact.

Some tribes have altogether abandoned the use of their traditional costumes because they are considered too plain, and have adopted others as their own, instead. The most popular but by no means the most attractive indigenous costume that is widely worn is the modern adaptation of the traditional Penampang attire. This is now known as the *Penampang Style,* which has greatly been influenced by the *sarong kebaya*. The costume of females consists of a long black skirt and a sleeveless blouse, and decorated with gold trimmings. The men wear black trousers and jackets with gold trimmings, and a headgear called *siga*. This headdress is an important article of local costume of men, that is worn or used by virtually all the indigenous groups in Sabah, irrespective of their culture and creed. It is a square piece of headcloth, handwoven or embroidered, and folded and tied according to styles representative of their district or group.

Cloth produced in the traditional manner, using the backstrap loom, are made from four types of yarn. The Dusun Tindal of Kota Belud extract fibre from a wild banana or *pisang lanut* (*Musa textilis*) which is processed into a coarse yarn for weaving their skirts, jacket and headwear. The Dusun of Kiulu also make a stiff cloth, made from *lamba*

(*Curculigo latifolia*) leaf fibre. Home-spun cotton from the locally cultivated *gapas* (*Gossypium herbaceum*) is still widely used by many tribes, particularly among the Rungus in the north, to make the cloth for various articles of clothing. The Bajau and Iranun of Kota Belud now buy imported plain cotton yarn called *gantian* which they dye according to the desired colours and stiffen with starch for weaving cloth.

The information and costumes illustrated in this book are based on the Sabah Museum costume collection. They cover seven indigenous communities, representing the three main categories of Austronesian peoples in Sabah. They are the Bajau and the Dusun Tindal of Kota Belud, the Kadazan of Papar, the Kadazan of Penampang, the Lotud of Tuaran, the Rungus of Kudat, and the Murut of Pensiangan. All seven groups of people live on the west and north coasts and the interior of Sabah. Each group wear costumes that are distinct in form, patterns, motifs and colour schemes that are both typical, and are characteristic of their respective tribe and district. At the same time, the differences in the costumes of the Dusun/Kadazan further indicate the richness and variety inherent in their material culture tradition. Culturally different groups who live in close proximity may also share many common elements in their traditional attire. This is evident among the Bajau and the Dusun Tindal of Kota Belud in the use of *kain saputangan*, the square handwoven cloth, for sashes and shoulder scarves.

The environment and people's view of life in the world around them often determine the nature of their material culture. Clothing is a basic human need. The evolution of what people wear usually mirror the social and environmental changes that are taking place in society. Costume has always reflected culture as much as culture has reflected costume. People will continue to change and adapt to new developments, and so will their costumes. Disappearing traditional skills and knowledge are being replaced with modern technology and commercial substitutes. Today's modern adapted forms may become tomorrow's traditions, as have so many of our traditional costumes. Those that have remain unchanged are museum collections preserved to provide a reference for the future. The costumes in this book present yet another aspect of Sabah's colourful cultural heritage and history.

PREPARING TEXTILES, COSTUMES AND ASSOCIATED ACCESSORIES FOR DISPLAY AT THE SABAH MUSEUM

Introduction

The objects in the exhibition "Colours, Cloth and Cosmos" are selections from the small but expanding collection of costumes and textiles of the Sabah Museum. While these represent only some of Sabah's many indigenous people, they illustrate the cultural diversity and richness of the State's heritage. The highlight of this exhibition are the textile objects which are the base of most of Sabah's indigenous costumes. The more elaborate costumes are worn on special occasions as ceremonial attire while the plainer ones are for daily wear.

Many of these costumes are made from more than one type of material and usually contain both organic and inorganic matter. The use of different materials to create the costumes is interesting but it causes certain problems for their long term care and preservation. Cloth, particularly those that are made from vegetable fibre, for instance, become subject to biological and other deterioration almost from the time they are made and used. Also, some costumes made of cotton or other plant fibre have shell and/or metal rings and buttons sewn on to the fabric or even woven into the cloth. Over time the shell may disintegrate, and the metals may corrode and stain the cloth. Thus, costumes and textiles may arrive at the Museum in any condition. Those that come in very badly soiled, torn, faded or stained need to be thoroughly cleaned, specially treated and repaired before they can be stored or displayed. Others in good condition may need only light cleaning. However, the Museum takes great care to acquire good pieces for its collection.

Acquisition of these costumes, textiles and associated accessories is carried out by the Ethnography Section which is also responsible for documentation and research of these objects. These objects are purchased in the field or in the Museum when local people bring in their heirlooms to sell. Many others are acquired through donations and sometimes through bequests. A special committee meets periodically to endorse these acquisitions and purchases.

The job of treating museum objects and ensuring their long term care and preservation for display and storage is carried out by the Conservation Section. While deterioration over time is inevitable for organic matter, the conservation staff take various preventive measures to arrest the problem. These include careful cleaning and treatment, handling and storage in a controlled environment for objects on display and in the stores.

Costumes and textiles especially those with colours require special attention. These have to be stored or displayed in humidity controlled and dust-free conditions, if possible with the minimum of light. If these objects are not carefully stored or displayed they may decay faster than the natural rate of deterioration. Not all of these objects are suitable for display. Some may be too fragile. Only the sturdier objects and fabrics are displayed in this particular exhibition.

Preparing textile objects for display

Documentation
↓
Condition Report
Photograph/Sketch
↓
Fumigation
Cleaning
↓
Repair
Packing
↓
Exhibition

The chart on the left gives an idea on the work and preparation required to mount a costume and textile exhibition. Depending on the scale of an exhibition, preparing textile objects for display may take two or more years.

(a) Documentation

All textile objects brought out for display from the store room are recorded in the Main Conservation

Registration Book and a Laboratory Number is given. The date of entry, the name, and details of the object are also recorded. (This is done with every artefact that enters the Conservation Section in order to record the movement of objects entering and leaving the Conservation Laboratory.)

(b) Condition Report

A report on the condition of the object is also made when it arrives at the Conservation Section. Details about the object regarding the damage and problems, as well as the materials used are noted. The information is needed to compare the condition of the object after it has been treated.

(c) Photograph/Sketch

Photographs are taken and sketches drawn of the object for detailed recording.

(d) Fumigation

After documentation, the object is fumigated to eliminate insects or any other micro-organisms which might be present in the fabric. This is a precaution to prevent contamination in the display. The date, chemicals, duration of treatment and method used are all recorded for future reference.

(e) Cleaning

After recording the details and fumigation, the textile object is ready to be cleaned. There are two ways to clean textile objects—the dry and wet methods. To determine which method is appropriate, a colour or pigment test is carried out. A wet method is suitable when the colours are stable, that is, they will not bleed in the cloth during cleaning.

(i) Dry Cleaning

In dry cleaning, no liquid is used to clean the textiles. A vacuum machine with low pressure is used to remove loose surface dust/dirt and the surface of textile must be covered with netting of some kind to prevent the fabric from being sucked into the vacuum machine. A soft bristle brush is usually used to loosen dust during cleaning. After this is done, the textile may be ready for exhibition or be packed and stored.

(ii) Wet Cleaning

The wet method is employed to clean robust textiles with stable colours or pigment. Sometimes water alone is sufficient to clean the textile and to remove stains. For stubborn stains, the following liquid detergents are used to remove them.

Synperonic-N: A fluid which contains nonylphenol with ethylene oxide, a wetting and dispersing agent used to remove dirt from textiles,

Vulpex Spirit Soap: A liquid cleaning agent based on potassium oleate mixed with methyl cyclohexanol and vulpex for more efficient removal of the dirt,

Textile Detergent: A liquid detergent which contains sodium tripolyphosphate and sodium carbonxymethyl cellulose.

These special detergents do not have the enzymes, bleach or brightening agents which normal washing soap has and are thus considered suitable for cleaning textile objects. However, the special detergents used in the cleaning process must be thoroughly rinsed out with deionized water.

Cleaned textiles are left to air-dry naturally in the shade as the high content of ultra-violet radiation in direct sunlight will cause colour to fade. After the textiles are cleaned and dried, they are repaired or mended, if necessary.

(f) Repair

Depending on the extent of damage, textile objects are repaired in many ways. Tears and missing areas are mended by hand-sewing a supporting structure (another piece of material) to the weak areas.

Weak fibres are consolidated with Paraloid B-72, an acrylic polymer-ethyl methacrylate co-polymer, and is a kind of resin which is soluble in acetone. When the acetone evaporates, the resin will solidify and form a "skin", to hold the weak fibres together. The aim is to reinforce the fibres so that the textile can withstand future handling.

(g) Packing

Textile objects in transit for display cases are sandwiched in acid-free tissue papers and if necessary carefully padded to minimise damage and contact with acidic materials which are destructive to organic fibre. Flat textiles are placed on rollers that are wrapped in acid-free materials. After treatment and repairs, direct contact with the objects and handling are minimised through the use of clean gloves and trays to provide maximum support for the object.

(h) Exhibition

Textile objects can be exhibited in many ways so long as the fibres are given the necessary support. Flat textiles are usually displayed on a piece of board or hung on a piece of wood covered with acid-free materials. Three-dimensional costumes are exhibited by using dummies or mannequins and other support.

The environment for the objects on display is also very important. The light intensity should remain below 50 lux for visible light and should not exceed 75 microwatts/lumen for ultra-violet radiation. Temperatures, especially within showcases, also should not exceed the range of 20°C–25°C. The relative humidity must remain constant between 50%–55% and frequent checks for any insect attack must be done. To prevent fading and deterioration in the display case, textile objects should be changed or rotated at least every three months.

The Bajau

The Bajau totalled 95,484 in 1975, constituting the second largest indigenous group in Sabah after the Dusun/Kadazan. Originally, they were seafarers of several kindred groups such as Iranun, Obian, Binadan, Suluk and other smaller minorities with similar cultural origins and customs.

Over the years, the Bajau people evolved into two distinct groups, with those on the west coast adopting sedentary agriculture such as rice farming, horse and cattle rearing as well as fishing. Those on the east coast are still coastal dwellers and are mainly fishermen.

The Bajau people are well known for their weaving and needlework skills. The Bajau women of Kota Belud make embroidered panels sewn into their long black wrap-skirt. The Bajau and Iranun of Kota Belud weave the traditional headgear called *kain dastar* which is also worn by almost every indigenous group in Sabah. The Binadan of Kudat is well known for their *kain pis* which is a richly embroidered one-metre piece of two-facing pieces of cloth.

Map of Sabah showing the distribution of the Bajau.

Photo: Sabah Museum

A Bajau lady in traditional costume. The unusual headgear is called *sarempak.*

Photo: Sabah Museum

A Bajau couple in traditional costumes.

TRADITIONAL COSTUME OF THE BAJAU

Costume of Women

badu sipak Brightly coloured satiny blouse, usually yellow. The flared sleeves show the cuffs of an underblouse in contrasting hue. The flared sleeves are two inches longer than the out-stretched arms and hands. Used for weddings. *Betawi* buttons in front, sometimes also on the sleeves.

badu sampit Brightly coloured long-sleeved satiny blouse, used for formal occasions.

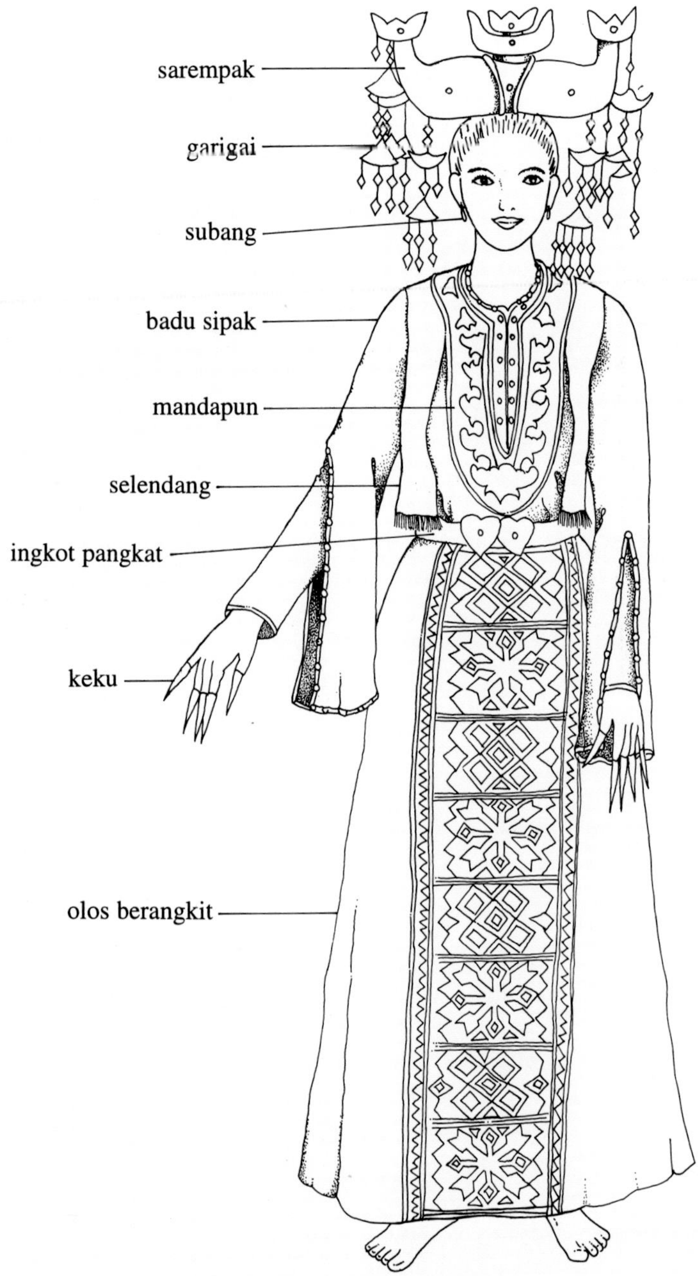

A Bajau lady in traditional costume.

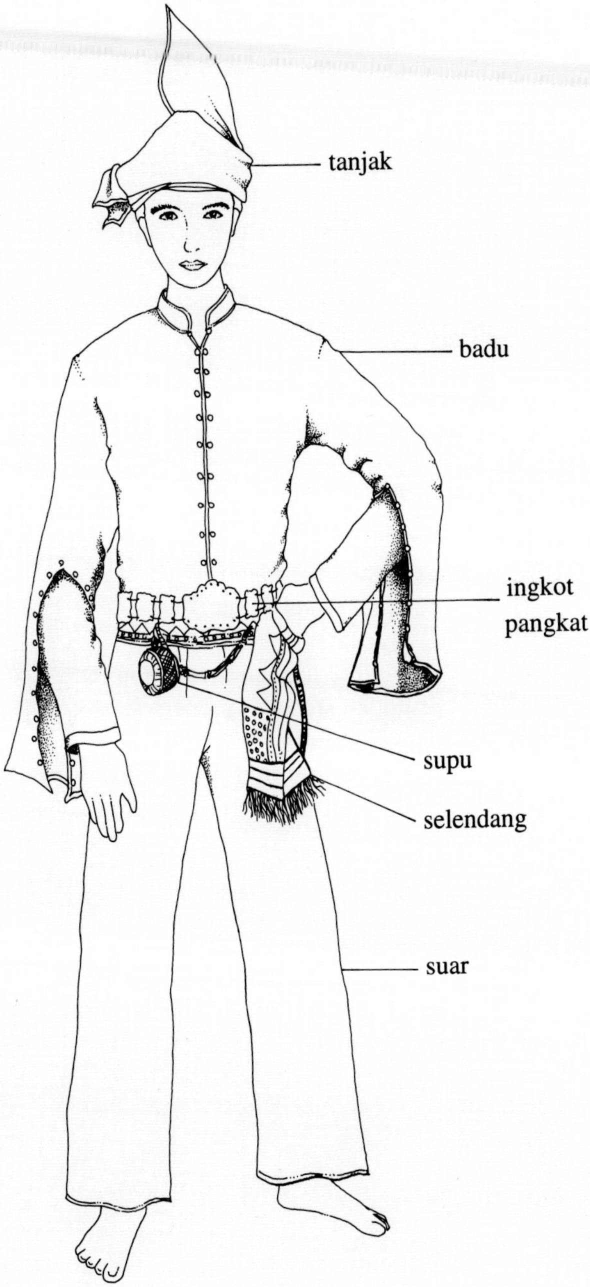

A Bajau man in traditional costume.

kain mogah Long handwoven wrap-skirt, with horizontal stripes, usually red and black, with supplementary weft motifs. Worn at weddings.

olos berangkit Full-length black wrap-skirt with a wide vertical panel of *berangkit* in front. The motifs are stylised: *bunga kapas* (cotton flower) and *pucuk rebung* (bamboo shoot). This exclusive wedding garment has become very rare nowadays.

selendang Scarf over the shoulders.

Accessories:

mandapun Flat cloth-covered collar-ornament accentuating the neckline decorated with stylized leaves in silver, goldleaf or substitute.

sarempak Two-piece head decoration in the shape of a ship made of gilded silver or modern substitute. Small ornaments dangling down from both ends are called *garigai*. The ornament is fitted around the hairbun on top of the head, three fingers away from the hairline.

galang Silver bangles.

subang Gold or silver ear pendants.

keku Long tapered, gold, silver or brass fingercovers worn by the bride.

ingkot pangkat Silver coin belt with a wide buckle.

Costume of Men

badu Brightly coloured satiny blouse, usually green, with flared sleeves showing cuffs of underblouse in contrasting hue. The flared sleeves are two inches longer than the out-stretched arms and hands. Used for weddings. *Betawi* buttons in front, sometimes also on the sleeves.

suar Trousers made of similar material in contrasting colour and red trimming. Black for weddings.

tanjak Headdress of folded *kain dastar* (used for weddings). *Podong*, used by horseman.

ingkot pangkat Silver coin belt with a wide buckle with an attachment called *supu* which is a round silver Bajau cigarette case.

selendang Sash tied around the waist.

Notes: The name *betawi* may refer to Batavia, present Jakarta and the former capital of the Dutch Indies. Similar buttons were in fashion in the Netherlands and are still part of some Dutch traditional costumes.

THE DUSUN TINDAL

The Dusun Tindal of Kota Belud number 240,096 in 1982. They are part of the larger Dusun/Kadazan group. They are mostly agriculturalists. The women are also skilled in producing homespun cloth made from *pisang lanut* (*Musa textilis*). The cloth is used to make their knee-length skirt (*gonob*) and women's headwear (*sunduk*). They also embroider on the hem of the skirt and the border of the headwear.

Apart from typically female items such as the headwear and skirt, the ceremonial costumes of Dusun Tindal men and women are identical. The slashed and flared sleeves of the shirt/blouse distinguish the Dusun Tindal costumes from the other Dusun groups. It is interesting to note that the Dusun Tindal who live in close proximity with the Bajau in Kota Belud both sport the slashed and flared sleeve feature in their costumes.

Map of Sabah showing the distribution of the Dusun Tindal.

A Dusun Tindal wedding couple in traditional costumes.

Traditional Costume of the Dusun Tindal, Kota Belud

Photo: Sabah Museum

Picture shows the back of a Dusun Tindal lady's traditional costume.

Costume of Women

sinipak Blouse of black velvet. The sleeves are slashed and flared at the elbows and lined with three layers of brightly coloured cloth trimmed with broderie. The upper part of the sleeves is decorated either with bands of *linangkit* or gold trimming, sequins, etc. *Betawi* buttons at front and sometimes also along the flared cuffs.

gonob Knee-length indigo dyed skirt traditionally made of *pisang lanut* (*Musa textilis*) with embroidered hem: red, yellow, white and green. The panels of skirt are joined with white stitch work. The vertical seam in front is decorated with embroidery in a zig-zag pattern. On the hem is sometimes a row of small brass bells.

lolopot Two sashes of *kain dastar* folded diagonally over the chest.

solindang Scarf folded over the shoulders.

sunduk Hood made of *pisang lanut* with embroidered border. Metallic beads and sequins. The *sunduk* is held in the hands during ceremonies.

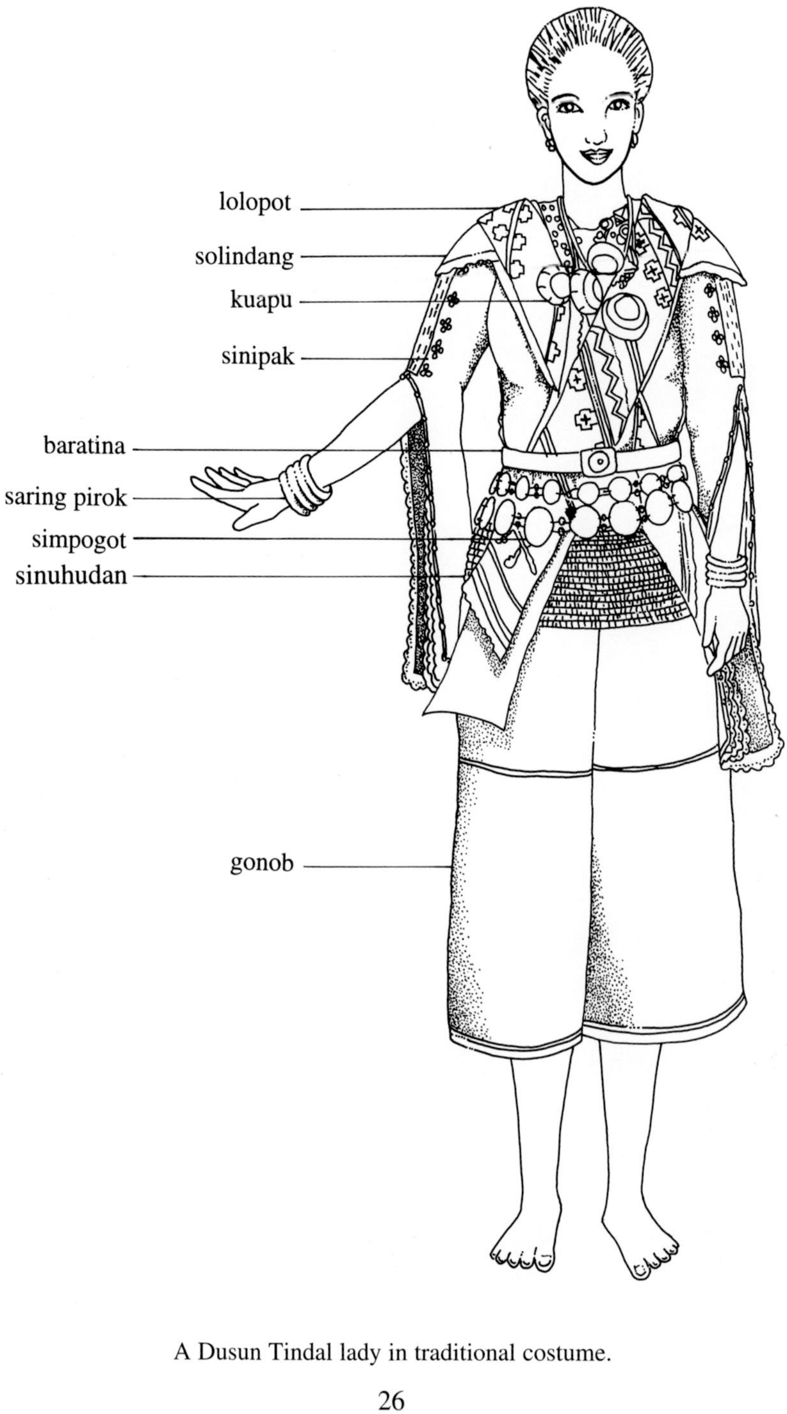

A Dusun Tindal lady in traditional costume.

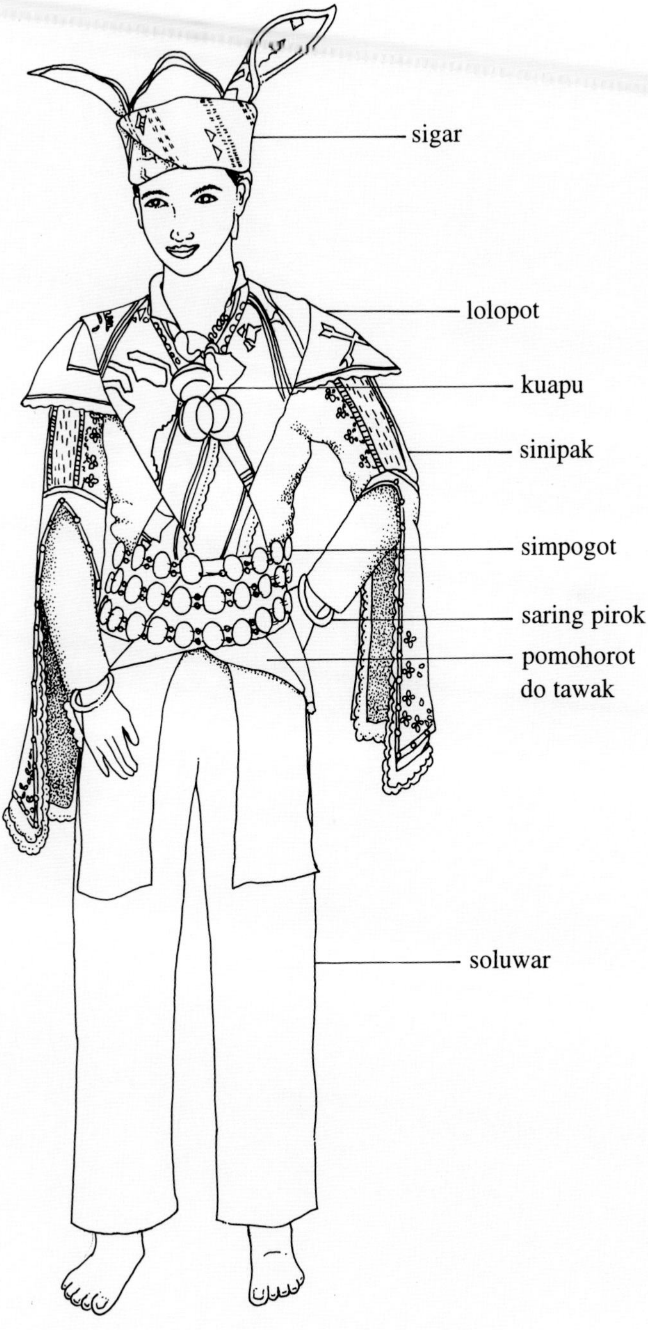

A Dusun Tindal man in traditional costume.

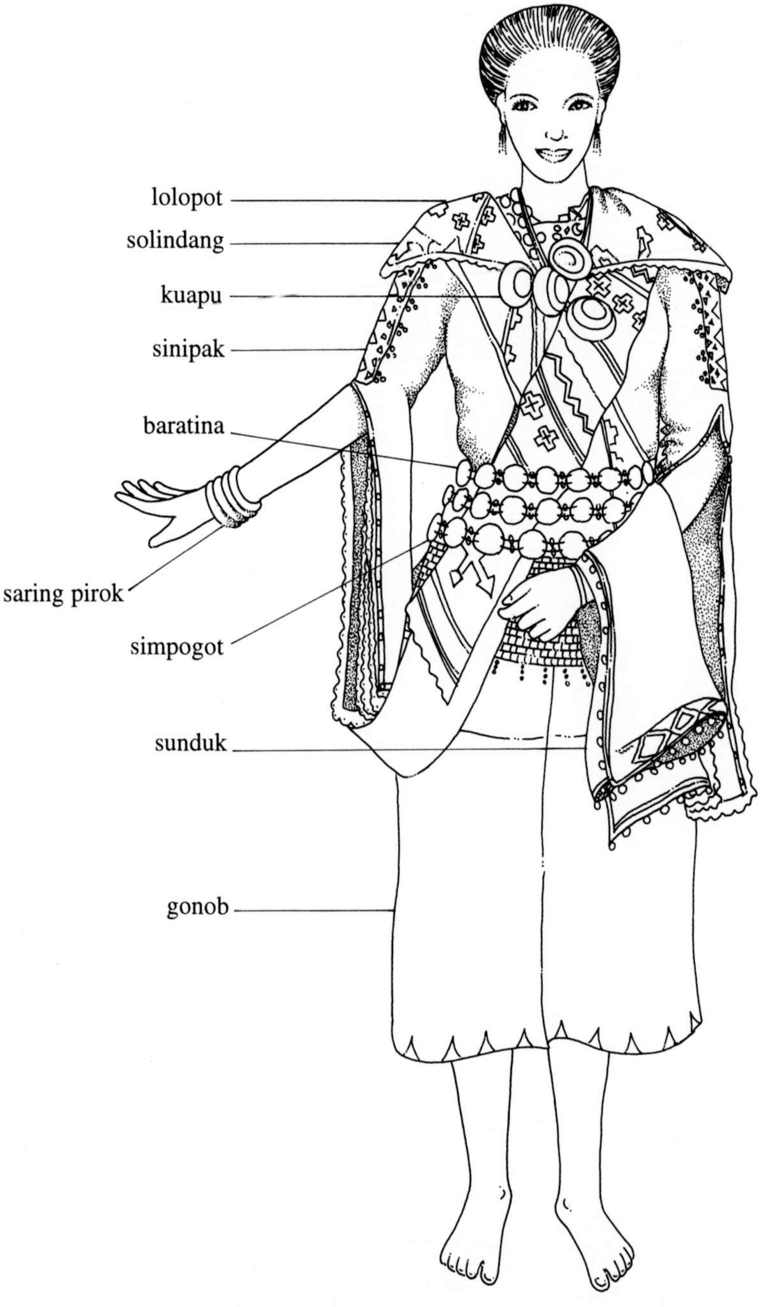

A Dusun Tindal lady in wedding attire.

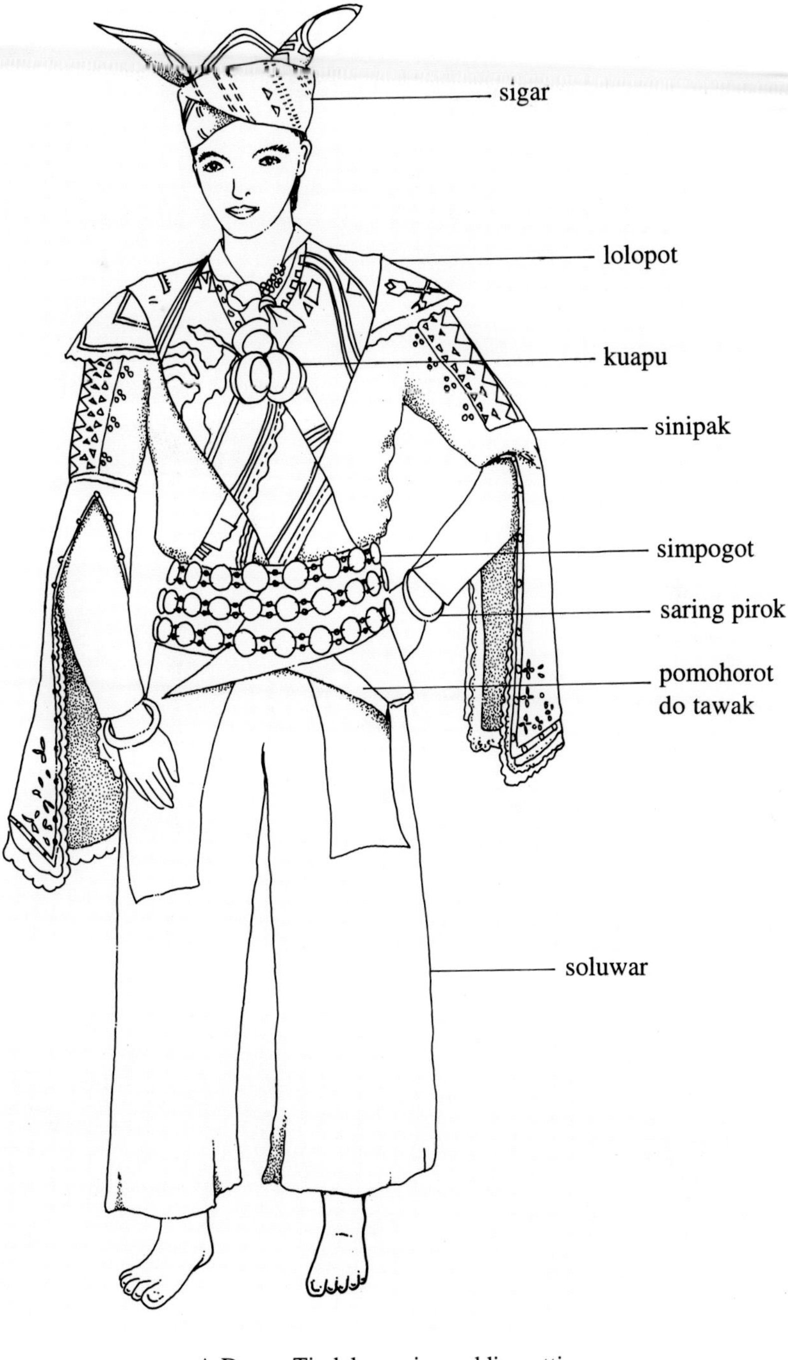

A Dusun Tindal man in wedding attire.

Accessories:

kuapu	An almost spherical embossed silver tobacco container made by the Bruneis. The shape may be derived from antique flat Dutch pocket watches. Two or three of these are worn around the neck on a silver chain.
baratina	Silver belt.
simpogot	Belt made of chained old silver coins (Straits Settlements, Hong Kong Dollars and Dutch Queen Wilhelmina Guilders). Worn below to *baratina*. The number of belts depends on the wealth of the wearer.
saring pirok	Silver bangles.
sinuhudan	Rows of old round beads forming a girdle around the hips. The heavy beads are strung with thick fibre but nevertheless the *sinuhudan* requires the wearer to walk about very carefully and sit down with even more caution.
kinokogis	Rows of small cylinder shell beads worn instead of the *sinuhudan*. Similar caution is needed to keep them from breaking.

Costume of Men

sinipak	Shirt of black velvet, usually worn over a long-sleeved shirt. The sleeves are slashed and flared at the elbows and lined with three layers of brightly coloured cloth trimmed with broderie. The upper part of the sleeves is decorated either with bands of *linangkit* or gold trimming, sequins, etc. *Betawi* buttons at front and sometimes also along the flared cuffs.
lolopot	Two sashes of *kain dastar* folded diagonally over the chest.

pomohorot do tawak Sash worn around the hips under the silver belt

soluwar Traditional trousers with wide waistline.

sigar Male headdress: traditionally folded *kain dastar*.

Accessories:

kuapu A round almost spherical silver tobacco container. Two or three of these are worn around the neck on a silver chain.

simpogot Belt made of chained old silver coins (Straits Settlements, Hong Kong Dollars and Dutch Queen Wilhelmina Guilders). Worn below to *baratina*, the number of coins depends on the wealth of the wearer.

saring pirok Silver bangles.

The Tuaran Lotud

The Lotud people are one of the Dusunic groups of Sabah. They number 5,000 to 6,000 in population and live in the Tuaran District about 30 km. north of Kota Kinabalu. They are mainly rice farmers. Traditionally, the work related to rice farming provides the cultural identity of a Lotud woman.

The women are also skilled in producing the embroidered panel called *linangkit* which is used to decorate the knee-length skirt, circular sash and trousers of their traditional costumes.

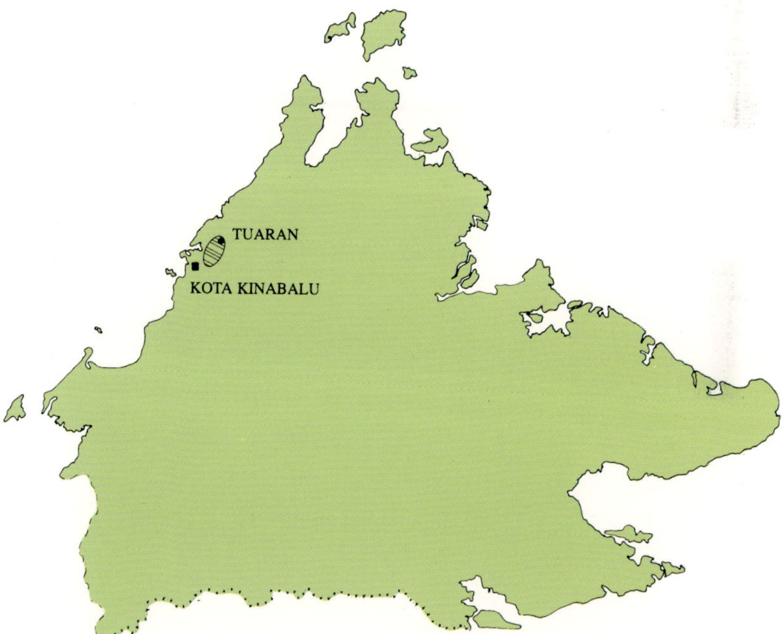

Map of Sabah showing the distribution of the Lotud.

Photo: Natural History Publications

Lotud *tantagas* in ceremonial attire.

(Right) Lotud man in traditional costume.

Photo: Sabah Museum

Photo: Benedict Topin/KDI

(Above) Picture shows the back of a Lotud woman's traditional costume.

(Below) A group of Lotud women in traditional costumes.

Photo: Sabah Museum

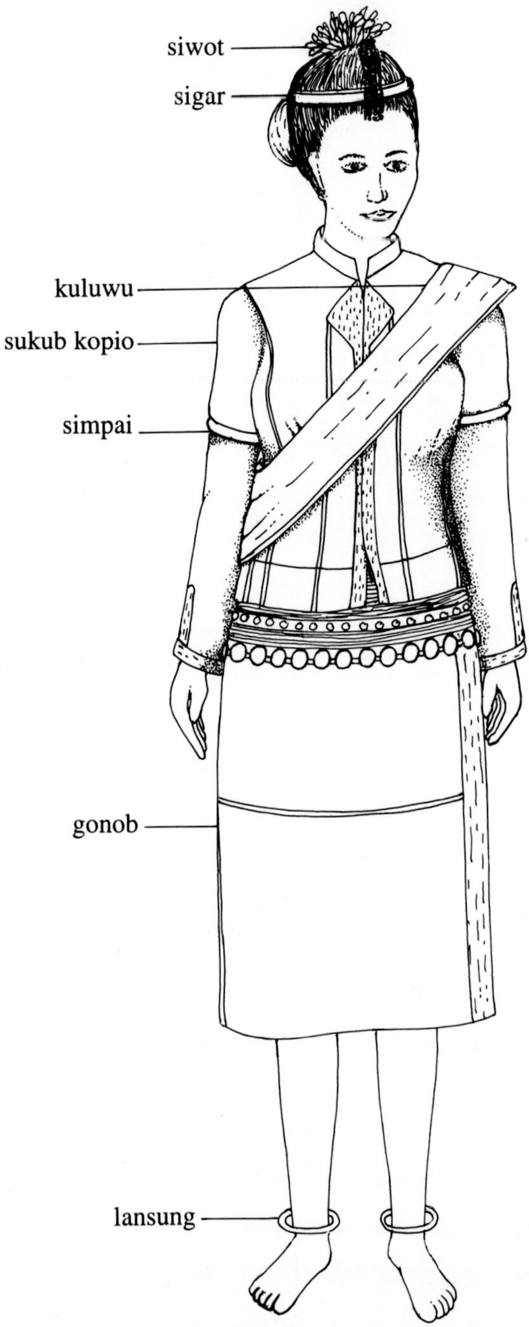

A Lotud lady in traditional costume.

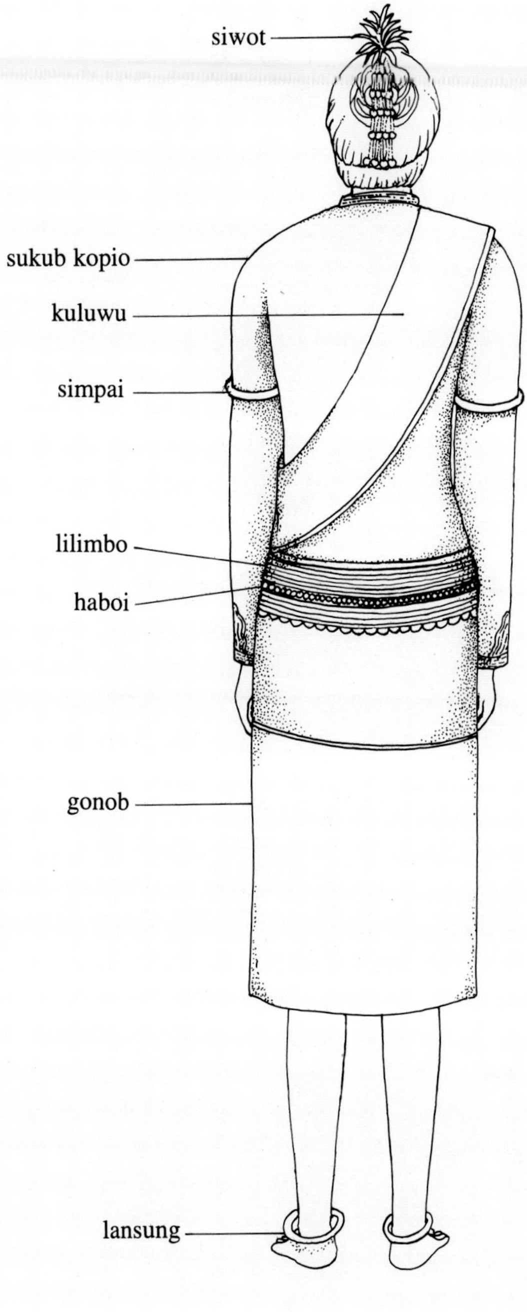

The back of a Lotud lady's traditional costume.

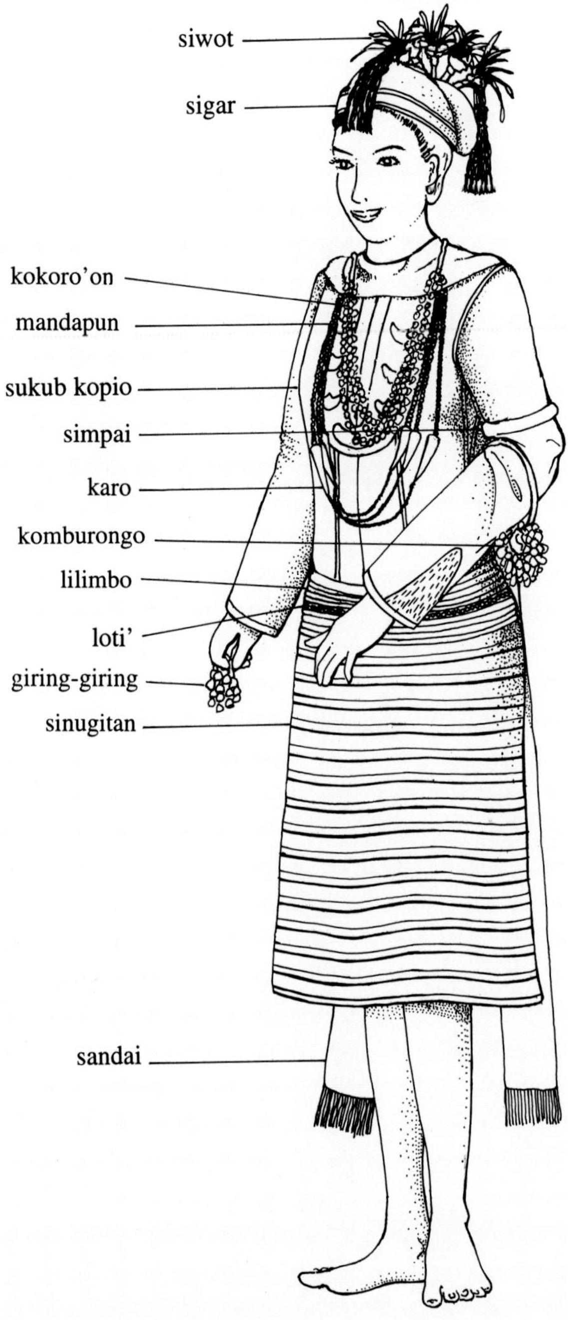

A Lotud *tantagas* in ceremonial attire.

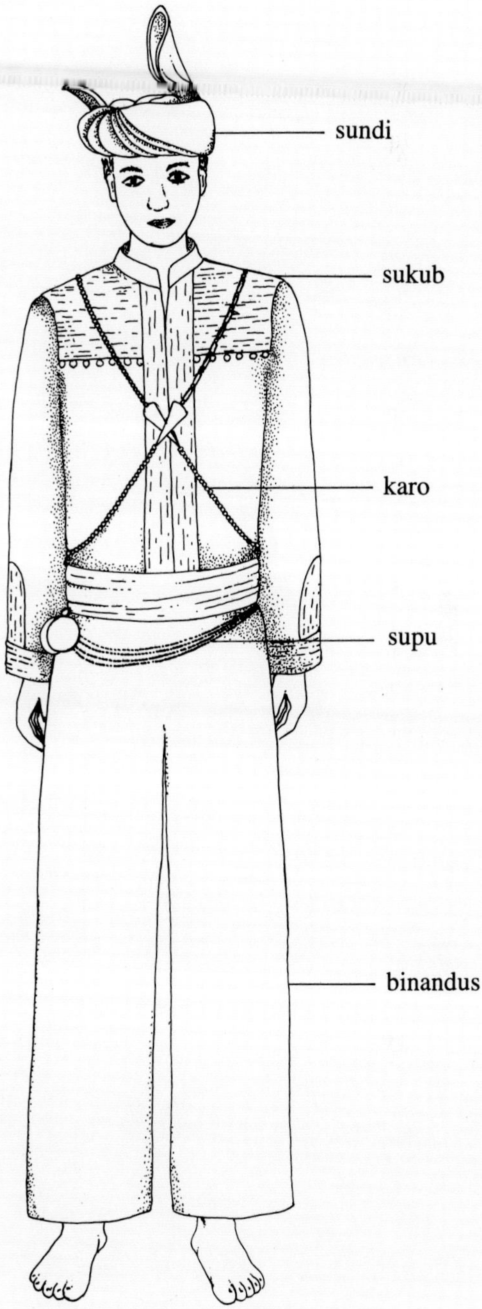

A Lotud man in traditional costume.

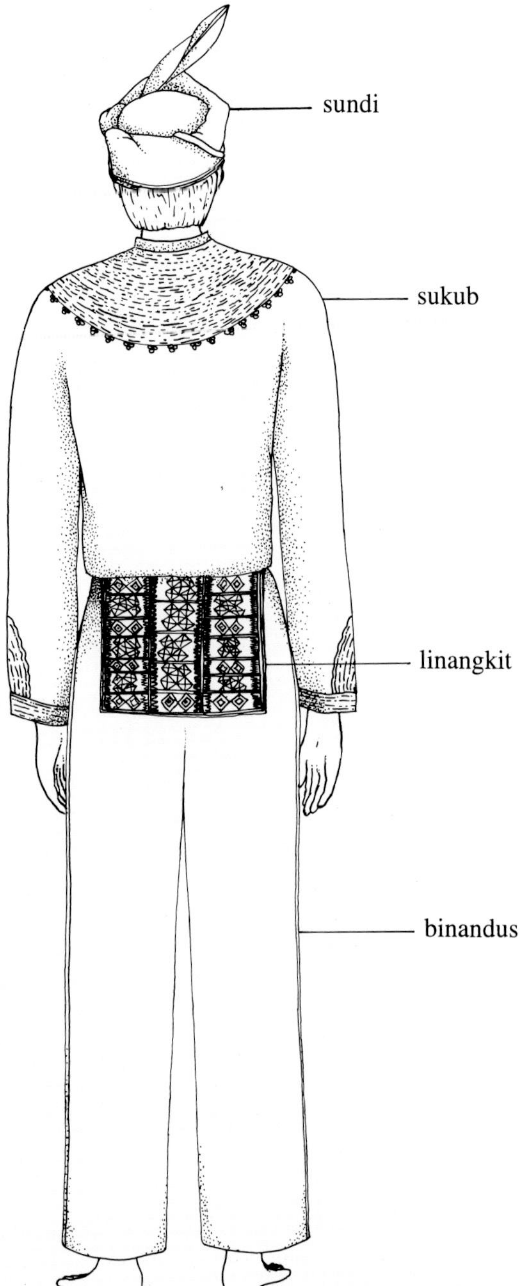

The back of a Lotud man's traditional costume.

TRADITIONAL COSTUME OF THE LOTUD, TUARAN

Costume of Women

Worn by the priestesses (*tantagas*) and other women during ceremonies, festive and social occasions.

sukub kopio Long-sleeved black cotton tailored blouse, with red *tinobogi* stitchwork at the seams. *Tinobogi* is a needle weaving technique of interlaced flanel stitches. A curvilinear motif of a bamboo shoot with sequins decorates the cuffs. The gold thread is "couched" onto the fabric. The *sukub* is closed with brooches of golden coins *(tombuku).*

gonob Knee-length black cotton tube skirt. Around the hips is a strip of *tinobogi* stitchwork and from the waist down a panel of *linangkit* needle work. The *gonob* is held up by a strip of white cloth (or *haboi*, *kain*). Sometimes, a batik *sarong* is worn over the short *gonob* to avoid exposure of the legs.

kuluwu Circular sash of black fabric, silk or synthetic, with gold trimming along the edges. At the seam a wide band of *linangkit*. During lengthy sitting-down ceremonies, the women may sling the circular *kuluwu* around their back and bend their knees to make the crouched position less tiring.

sinugitan Knee-length dark coloured skirt worn by the *tantagas.* Made from cotton, the cloth is very old, the material likely to have been imported a long time ago.

Accessories:

lilimbo Wide girdle of interconnected loops of split rattan, worn around the hips. The colour of the rattan signifies the status of the wearer, i.e., red for childless women, red and black for mothers.

loti A white cotton strip with a chain of small silver coins (*loti*) running over the middle of the *lilimbo*.

haboi Silver dollar belt. Lotud women wear only one *haboi*.

porotina Silver belt with a diamond-shaped clasp made by the Brunei.

sigar Headband with red rattan rims. The narrow band is decorated with rectangular or square plates of embossed goldleaf or modern substitute. The hairbun hangs over the *sigar*.

siwot Ornament for the head which is stuck into the hairbun. It consists of four bunches of red cloth and black cock feathers. Nowadays gathered in badminton shuttles. Strings of silver-green beads with bits of red cloth dangle over the forehead from the first bunch, and downward from the last one. The silver-green beads are a modern substitute for the iridescent wings of beetles that were used in the old days. It is worn during ceremonies.

mandapun Stiff ornamental collar of red cotton with embossed gold or silver plate shaped as leaves, made by the Brunei.

simpai Upper arm bracelet of hollow embossed silver.

lansung Hollow embossed silver anklets. In the old days, the *lansung* were of solid brass made by the Rungus.

karo A necklace made of mostly long barrel beads of glass, shell and carnelian. In between these are hollow silver beads and concave ornaments over a wooden base. Usually two or three *karo* are worn together. The cone-shaped ornaments are arranged symmetrically with the points downwards.

lontugion Big *karo*: set of two necklaces worn crossed over the chest.

giring-giring A set of approximately 12 brass slit bells used by the *Tantagas* (female ritual specialists) during ceremonies.

tutubik A praying device made of turtle bone, used by the *Tantagas* during ceremonies.

sandai Long sash draped over one shoulder to the front and over the next shoulder falling to the back.

kokoro'on Necklace of small glass coloured beads. A few are normally worn by the *tantagas.*

komburongo Used in ritual ceremonies by the *tantagas*, it is a small pottery jar [usually of the Ching period (1645–1911)] with a cloth-covered rattan handle, containing ritual plants and animal bones. The container is looped over the lower part of the arm. Decorative beads adorn the jar.

Costume of Men

sukub Black cotton shirt with similar decoration as the women's blouse.

binandus Trousers with a square piece of *linangkit* at the backside just under the waist. Older trousers have a very wide waist band.

sundi — *Kain dastar* headdress, folded in different ways. When two points stick out, the wearer has two wives and so on.

supu — A silver chain with an attached round silver tobacco container, worn around the waist.

THE MURUT

The Murut is the third largest indigenous group in Sabah comprising subgroups such as the Baukan, Gana', Kalabakan, Okolod, Paluan, Selungai, Serudung, Tagal, Timugon and the Beaufort and Keningau Murut. They inhabit the interior and south-eastern parts of Sabah and the territory straddling the Kalimantan and Sarawak borders. They are mostly shifting cultivators and hunters with some riverine fishing. Their staple food is tapioca. According to the census in 1977, the Muruts totalled nearly 40,000 people.

The Murut costume for men comprised a jacket made of tree bark *Artocarpus tamaran*, a red loincloth and a headdress also made of tree bark decorated with Argus pheasant feathers. The costume for women is a short, black, sleeveless blouse and a long, black skirt decorated with colourful beads.

Map of Sabah showing the distribution of the Murut.

Photo: Sabah Museum

Photo: Sabah Museum

(Above) A group of Murut ladies in traditional costumes. (Below) Showing the backs of their costumes.

Photo: Benedict Topin/KDI

Murut girls in their traditional costumes.

Photo: Sabah Museum

A Murut man in traditional costume.

Photo: Benedict Topin/KDI

(Above) Murut headgears with Argus pheasant feathers.

Photo: Benedict Topin/KDI

(Left) Two Murut men in their traditional costumes.

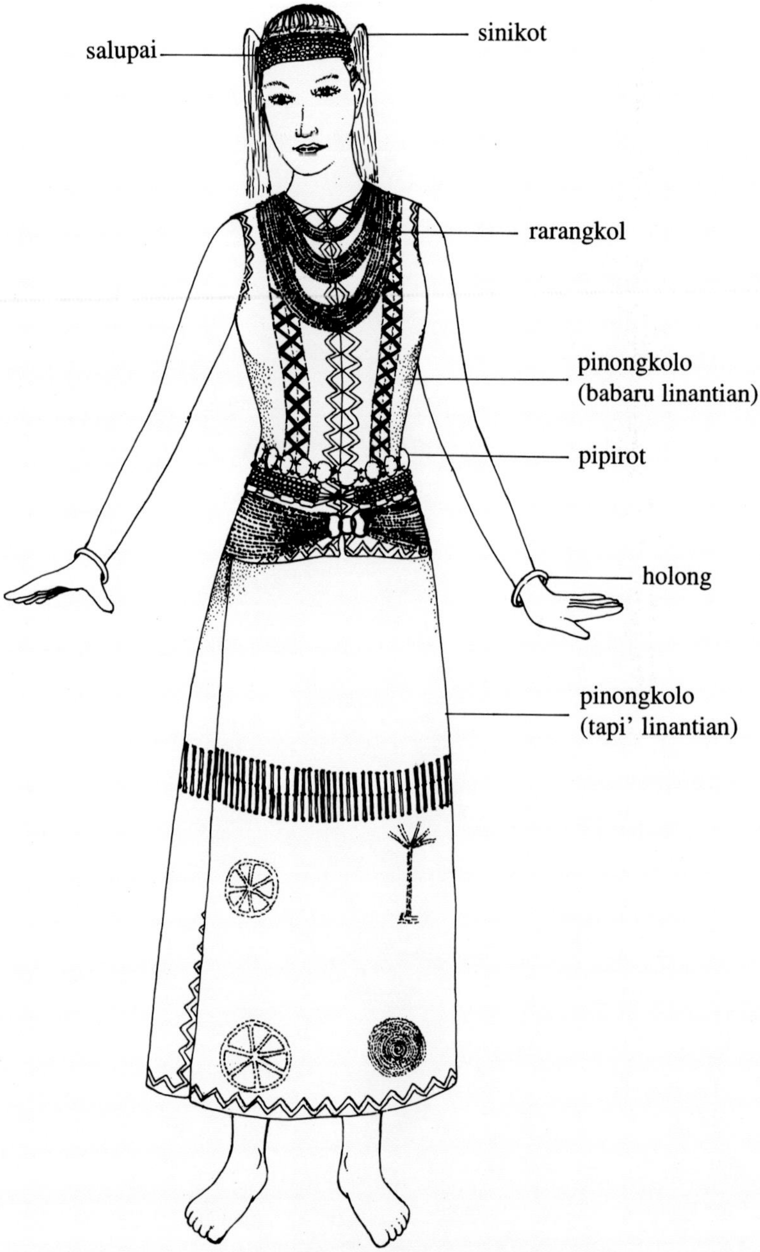

A Murut lady in traditional costume.

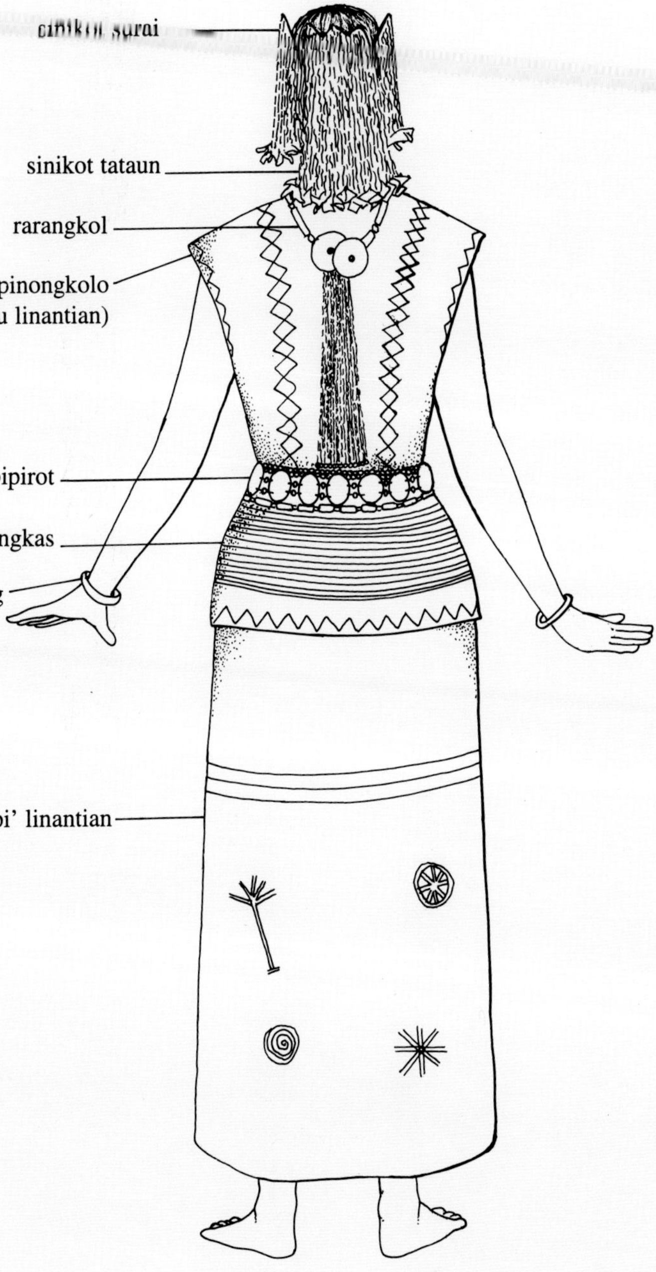

The back of a Murut woman's traditional costume.

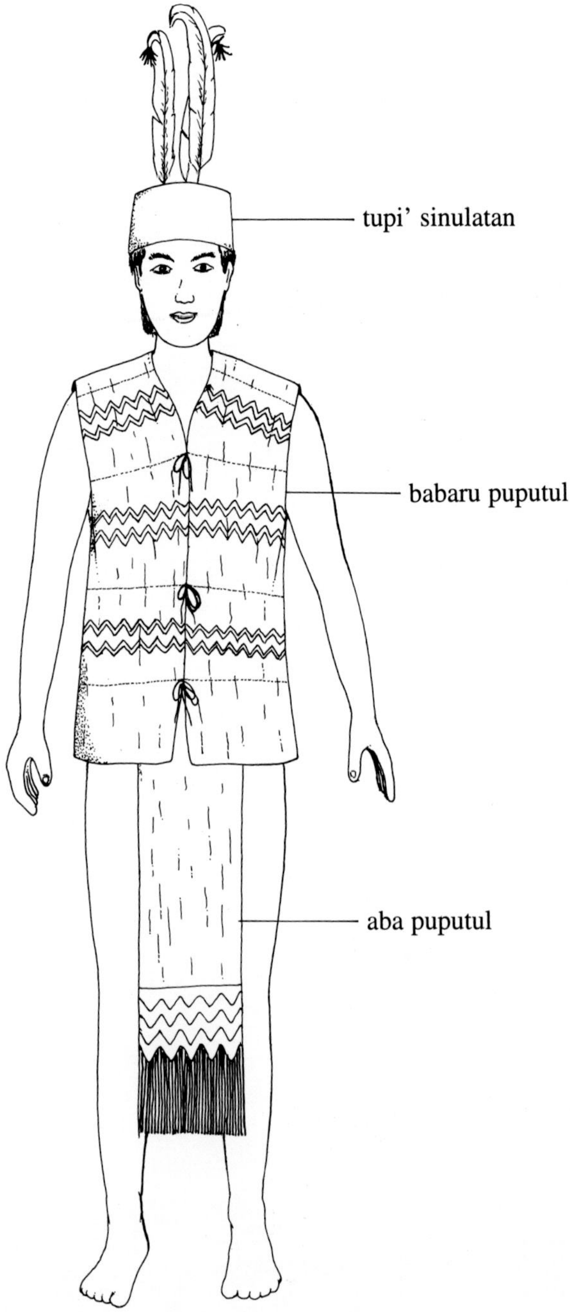

A Murut man in traditional costume.

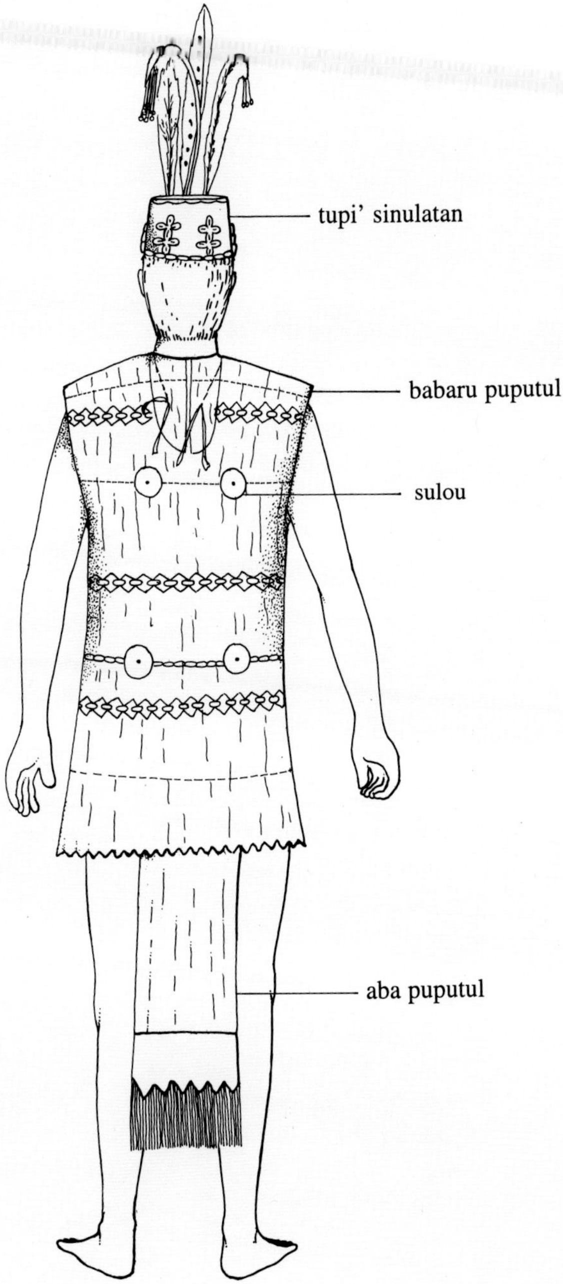

The back of a Murut man's traditional costume.

TRADITIONAL COSTUME OF THE MURUT

Costume of Women

pinongkolo Traditional costume of women comprising a blouse and a long wrap-skirt of black cotton, and decorated with beadwork. The decorated blouse is called *babaru linantian* and the wrap-skirt *tapi' linantian*.

pipirot Belts/waist bands of silver coins *(pipirot linggit)* and various types of beads; most popular being the *aki' nampalur, kotos, bungkas, aki'*, and *olod*.

salupai A headdress of several rows of beads. When there are many strings, they are shaped into a round skullcap. The *salupai* functions as a support for the *sinikot*.

sinikot A set of three hairpins, with the *sinikot tataun* in the middle and two *sinikot surai* on both sides of the hairbun. The larger *sinikot tataun* has the longest strings of tiny beads floating downwards to the middle of the back.

rarangkol Necklaces of various types of beads usually in a certain order—according to length: *bungkas, kotos, aki' pangungupu', bulul, olod,* etc.

holong A pair of bracelets. If made from shell (probably the shell of the giant sea clam), they are called *holong sulou*. Any type of round beads may be strung together as an alternative.

Costume of Men

babaru puputul Bark vest. The bark comes from the *puputul* tree *(Artocarpus kunstleri)*. It is cut length wise to fashion sleeveless jackets and loincloths. The material of the jackets is strengthened with transverse darning. Formerly, the fibre of pineapple leaves was used. It may be decorated with simple beadwork motifs.

aba puputul Loincloth of approximately two metres long; made of inner bark of the *puputul* tree. The fabric is passed between the legs and wound around the waist.

Modern cotton *aba* (*aba ra kain*) are cut as shorts with lengths of cloth attached to front and back, more or less like apron. Red cloth is common because red is used to symbolise bravery. Cotton applique of zig-zag motifs (*rinda-rinda* or *rinipon kapit*).

tupi' sinulatan Headband of tree-bark decorated with feathers, preferably of the *tuwou* (Argus pheasant), or a pair of *sinikot*.

Some stylized motifs on Murut traditional costume

sinusu' Peacock neck feathers

linimburu Leech-like motif

tinukaang Zig-zag/tips of leaves of the *puputul* tree arranged in a row

sinuli bamboo slats flooring

kalayam manuk chicken feet-like motif

sinusulou *sulou*-like motif (*sulou* = the giant sea clam)

mato nu orou sun-like motif

THE PAPAR KADAZAN

In 1991, the Papar Kadazan number 36,688. They are part of the larger Dusun/Kadazan group. They are mostly agriculturalists who live in the Papar District.

The women wear a distinct costume—a conical hat of fine bamboo strips, a knee-length skirt with a horizontal and a vertical strip of cross-stitched panel lined with gold thread, and a short jacket with *Betawi* buttons over a white blouse. The conical hat which features coloured feather-downs or artificial flowers at the top shows the wearer's marital status—feather-downs for the single lady and flowers for the married woman. A widow, grandmother or elderly woman wears neither feather-downs nor flowers on her hat.

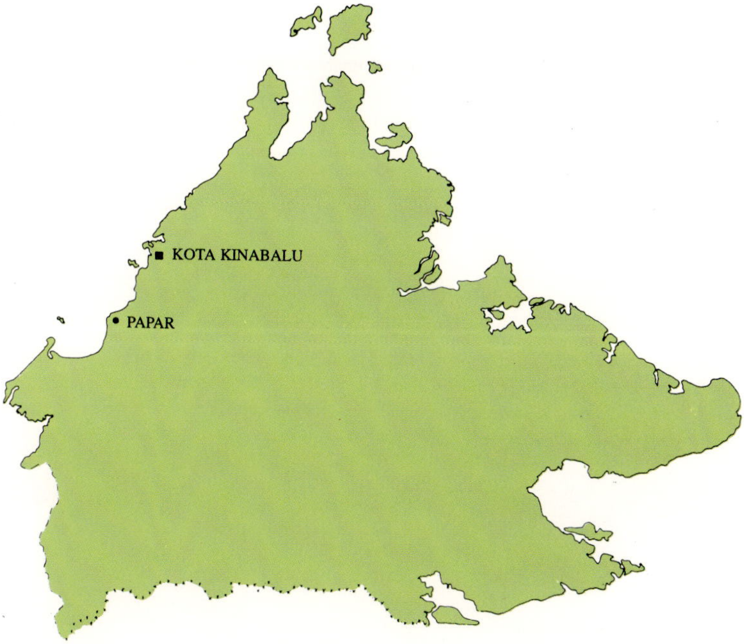

Map of Sabah showing the distribution of the Papar Kadazan

Photo: Sabah Museum

Photo: Sabah Museum

The front and back view of a Papar Kadazan lady in traditional costume.

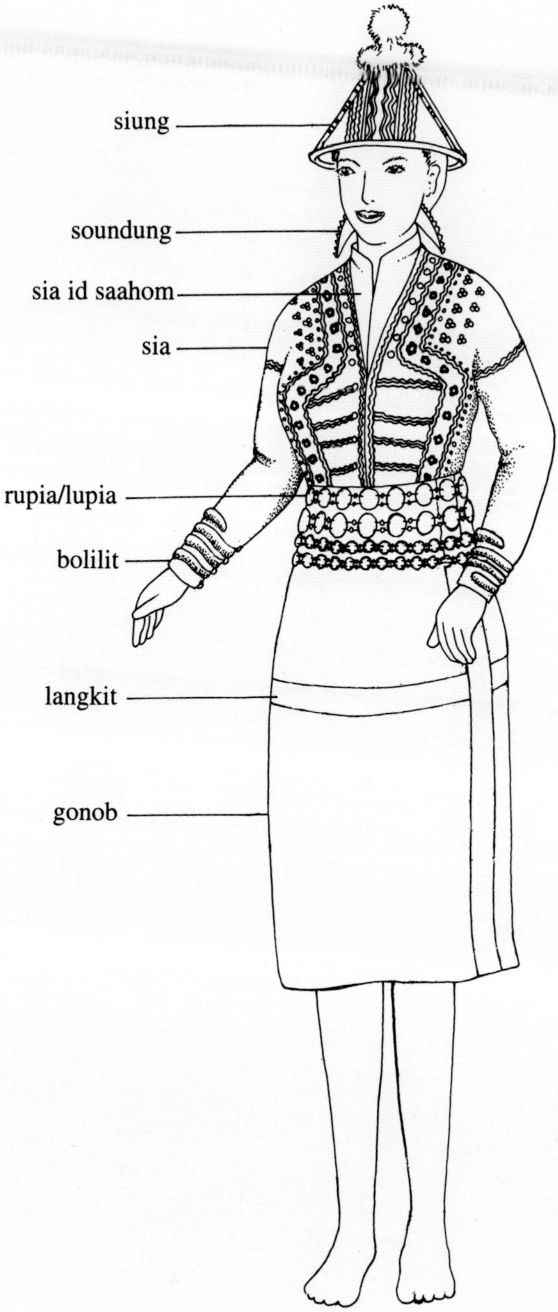

A Papar Kadazan lady in traditional costume.

A Papar Kadazan man in traditional costume.

Traditional Costume of the Papar Kadazan

Textile

Basic material: Black cloth, generally velvet, gold trimming (*palada*).

Costume of Women

sia	Short jacket with large *Betawi* buttons *(kubamban)* of brass or modern substitute along the neckline and smaller ones *(tombohu)* on the cuffs. Gold trimming on the seams. The sequins on the sleeves are a modern addition. Under the jacket a white blouse *(sia id saahom)* is worn.
gonob	Knee-length skirt with a horizontal and a vertical strip of *langkit* cross-stitched lined with gold thread.
siung	Conical hat of very fine bamboo strips with three decorative zones running to the top: patterns in red and black. Tufts of (coloured) feather-downs or artificial flowers on top.
soundung	Scarf worn under the *siung*.
bolilit	Flat silver bracelet shaped like a spiral.
rupia/lupia	Silver "dollar" (British trade dollar) belt: unmarried ladies wear four *lupia/rupia* and married women wear two *lupia/rupia*.

Costume of Men

sia	Long-sleeved jacket with gold trimming.
souva	Trousers with gold trimming.
sigal	Headdress of folded *kain dastar*.

THE PENAMPANG KADAZAN

The Kadazan people of the Penampang District is a subgroup of the Dusun/Kadazan group. They are traditionally farmers practising wet rice cultivation with some hunting and riverine fishing. According to the Kadazan Dusun Cultural Association, there are about 300,000 Kadazan speakers.

Generally, the trimmings and embroidery on the Kadazan costume are simple and dignified in comparison with other ethnic groups. The men's jacket and trousers bear some Chinese influence.

There are three different styles of blouses for the women. One is a blouse with short sleeves worn by young ladies. Another is a blouse with 3/4 sleeves worn by middle-aged ladies for daily or casual use. The third one is worn by elderly women and female ritual specialists/priestesses during ceremonies.

Map of Sabah showing the distribution of the Penampang Kadazan.

Photo: Sabah Museum

A group of Penampang Kadazan men and women in traditional costumes.

Photo: Natural History Publications

Elderly Penampang Kadazan women in traditional costumes.

Photo: Benedict Topin/KDI

Penampang Kadazan priestesses.

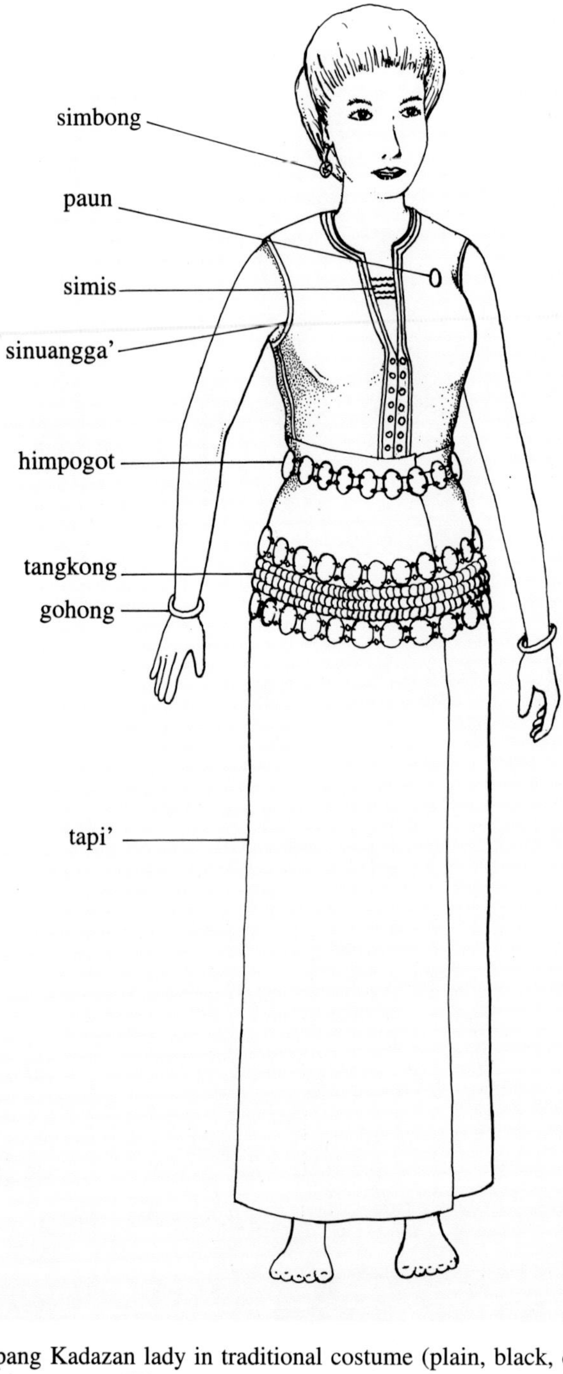

A Penampang Kadazan lady in traditional costume (plain, black, cotton, long-wrap-skirt).

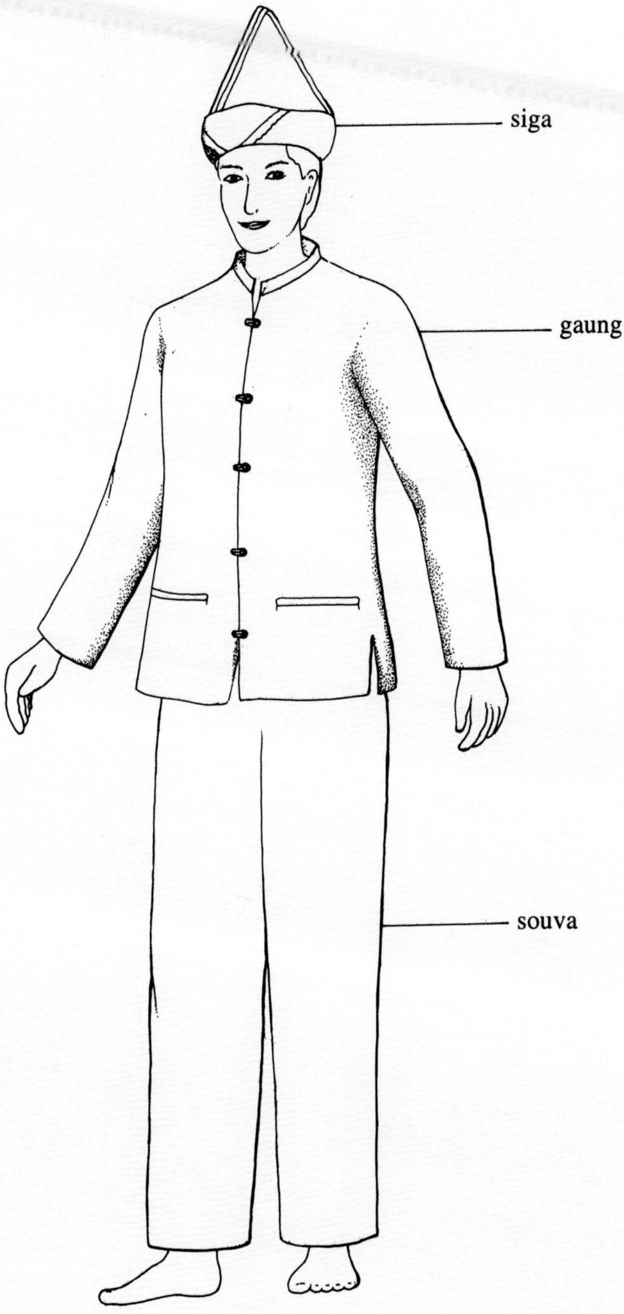

A Penampang Kadazan man in traditional costume (long-sleeved shirt without embroidery).

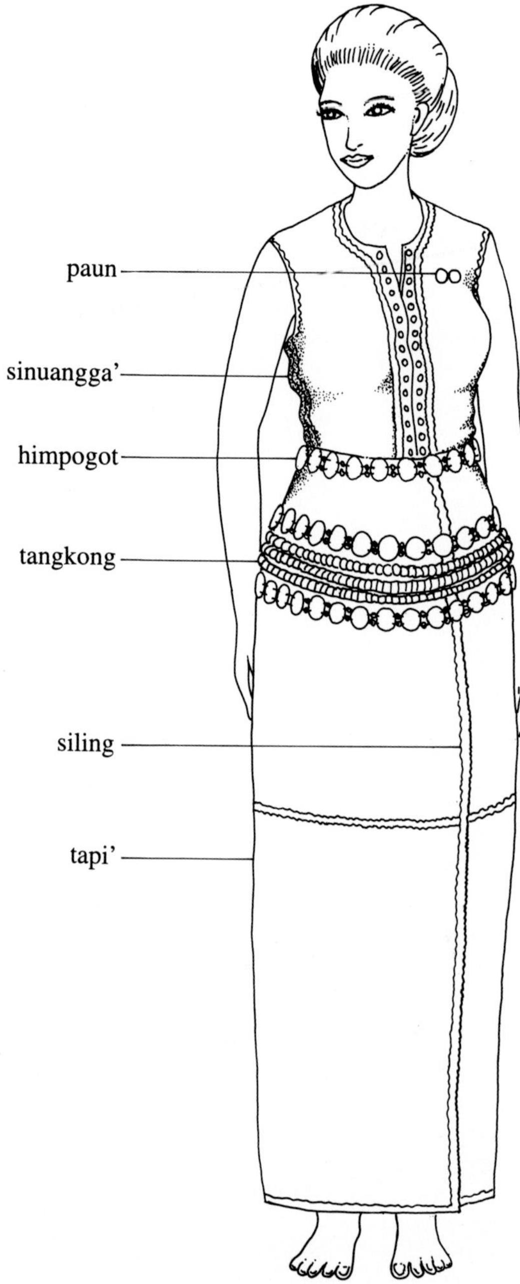

A Penampang Kadazan lady in traditional costume decorated with gold trimmings.

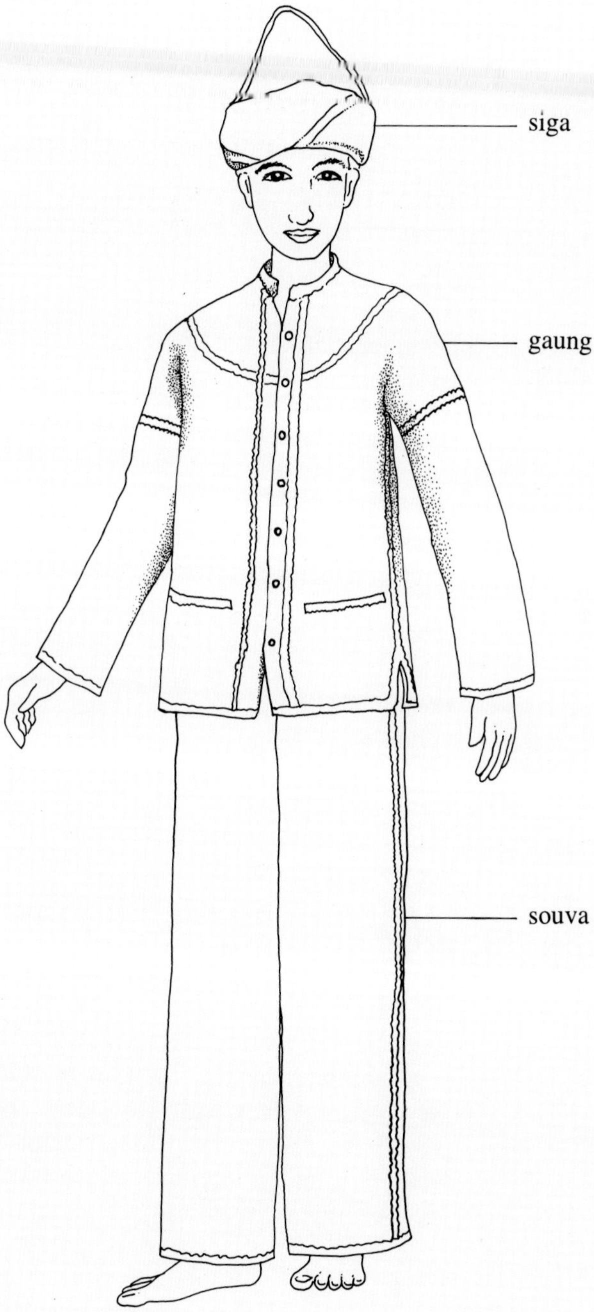

A Penampang Kadazan man in traditional costume (long-sleeved shirt decorated with gold trimmings and gold buttons).

Traditional Costume of the Penampang Kadazan

Textile

Basic material: Black commercial fabric: silk or velvet for ceremonial occasions, cotton (vernacular *tuit*) for daily wear.

Costume of Women

sinuangga' Blouse with short sleeves and U-neck worn by younger women.

Sober embroidery along the opening for head and arms, and along the seams at the sides and along the middle of the back: red, yellow and cream cotton yarn. Main stitches: *sinusuk bulus* (chain stitch), *tantop* (flanel stitch). A flanel stitch technique is also used to make *binuunsi',* a narrow band of needle weaving in red and yellow looking somewhat like shoelace.

Betawi buttons are looped through a string on the inside. This way, the valuable buttons can be used for various blouses. *Betawi* buttons used to be fixed all the way up to the neck for ceremonial occasions and half way up from the lower end of the blouse for daily wear. Nowadays, this appears not to be differentiated. The buttons are tied together from the top down to the bottom of the blouse with a cotton thread.

The gold-plated silver *Betawi* buttons were a status symbol for the Kadazan Penampang. If one could afford a set of thirty buttons *(sonsolobuan),* one was considered a wealthy person.

sinompukung Blouse with 3/4 sleeves. No embroidery. Usually worn over the *sinuangga'* like a jacket when the wearer goes out of the house, such as to visit a friend.

Nowadays, the *sinompukung* is often embroidered and worn by older women as a blouse instead of as a jacket as in the olden days.

kihongon Blouse with long sleeves, worn by elderly women and female ritual specialists/priestesses or *Bobohizan* during ceremonies. The embroidery is similar to the one on the *sinuangga'*.

simis "Chemise"—a white cotton underblouse. Sometimes just a white kerchief is tucked into the U-neck.

tapi' Long cylindrical wrap-skirt, formerly of plain black cotton. Nowadays often enlivened with *siling*: gold trimming, running over the hips, in front of the skirt, crossed by another band of trimming from the waist down.

Accessories:

himpogot Silver "dollar" belt. A maximum of three are used depending on personal wealth, one around the waist and the other two above and below the *tangkong*.

tangkong Hip-belt of approximately 84 embossed brass rings on rattan strings *(hindavog)*. Three *tangkong* are worn together, alternately strung with red *(hindagang)*, black *(initom)* and red rattan strings for unmarried girls and all black for married women. The string is always "bare" somewhere at the back to avoid *asampon* (lack of breathing space). Later in life the *tangkong* arc stretched out for various reasons, one of which is so that it is easier to carry a back basket.

titimbok Hairpin to decorate and fasten the hairbun.

tiningkokos Brass or silver spiral bracelet.

gohong Brass or silver bracelets.

hamai Necklace.

simbong Earrings.

paun Brooch of gold coin(s).

siga do bobohizan Worn during rituals/ceremonies by the *Bobohizan.* It is an ornate headdress that is made from feathers of peacocks or turkeys. The plumage is tightly packed together and sewn onto a wide band of cloth. The feathers form the support and shape of the headdress, which when seen from the front is almost wholly covered with the cloth that fans outwards from the head. From the back however, these feathers are almost wholly visible. The wide band of cloth to which the feathers are sewn is decorated with multicoloured applique, embroidery and beads. *Andavi do tandaa'* or long-tailed feathers of roosters are also sewn at the front of the cloth. The tip of each of these feathers is tied with several small pieces of colourful cloth. From the lower part of both sides of the headdress are sewn several long loops of coloured beads which hang down to the front/chest. The headdress is secured/tied by cloth at the back of the head. The headdress is approximately one and a half feet in height.

husob A colourful cloth worn by the *Bobohizan* over one shoulder and across the body. Usually two *husob* are worn together criss-crossing each other.

Costume of Men

gaung Long-sleeved shirt without embroidery. Nowadays it is decorated with gold trimming and gold buttons.

souva Black trousers with wide indigo-blue waistband. Gold trimming on the seams along the hips for modern trousers.

kaking or ***toogot*** Black waist sash.

siga Headcover of handwoven *kain dastar*, folded or twisted in a number of distinctive ways:

Hinopung (hopung = python): twisted model
Kinahu' (kahu' = potholder): folded model
Sinimbitan or *tinahanuk*: only one small corner sticking out.

tupi' sinikat Circular hat of sturdy string made with the coil and tie technique to support the *siga*.

THE RUNGUS

The Rungus is a sub-group of the Dusun/Kadazan group found mainly on the Kudat and Bengkoka peninsula in the northern part of Sabah. According to the 1981 census, the Rungus number about 40,000.

They are sedentary farmers as well as shifting cultivators. Their staple food is rice and maize. They are skilled in producing homespun cloth made from cotton—*kapok,* for their costumes. They also produce handicrafts made from a variety of materials, bead necklaces and other accessories.

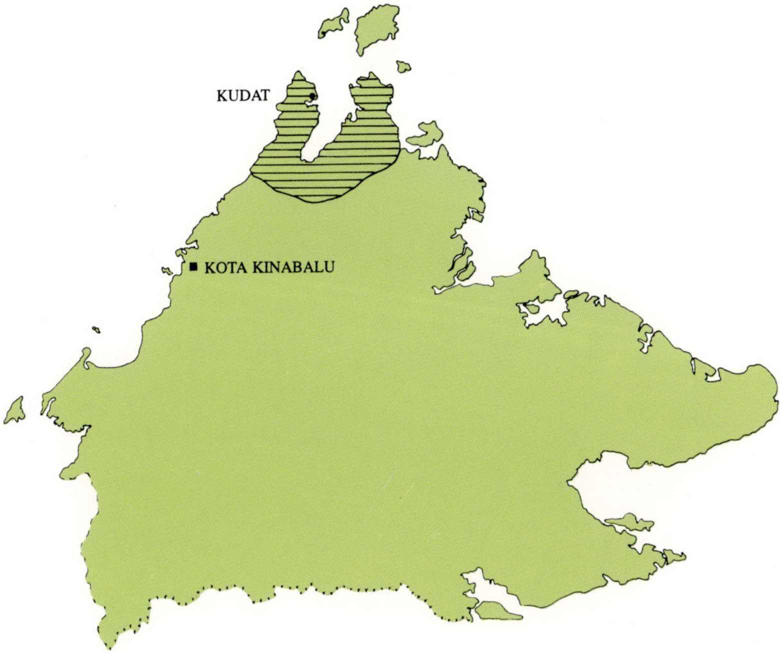

Map of Sabah showing the distribution of the Rungus.

(Left) A Rungus girl in traditional attire.

Photo: C.L. Chan

Photo: David Lee/KDI

Photo: Benedict Topin/KDI

(Above left) The back costume of a Rungus lady. (Above right) A Rungus girl in her traditional costume.

(Left) A Rungus man in traditional costume.

(Below) Showing the backs of a Rungus couple's traditional costumes.

Photo: Sabah Museum

Photo: Sabah Museum

Photo: Benedict Topin/KDI

The front costume of a Rungus man. The headgear is called *sigal.*

Photo: Benedict Topin/KDI

Close up of the front costume of a Rungus man.

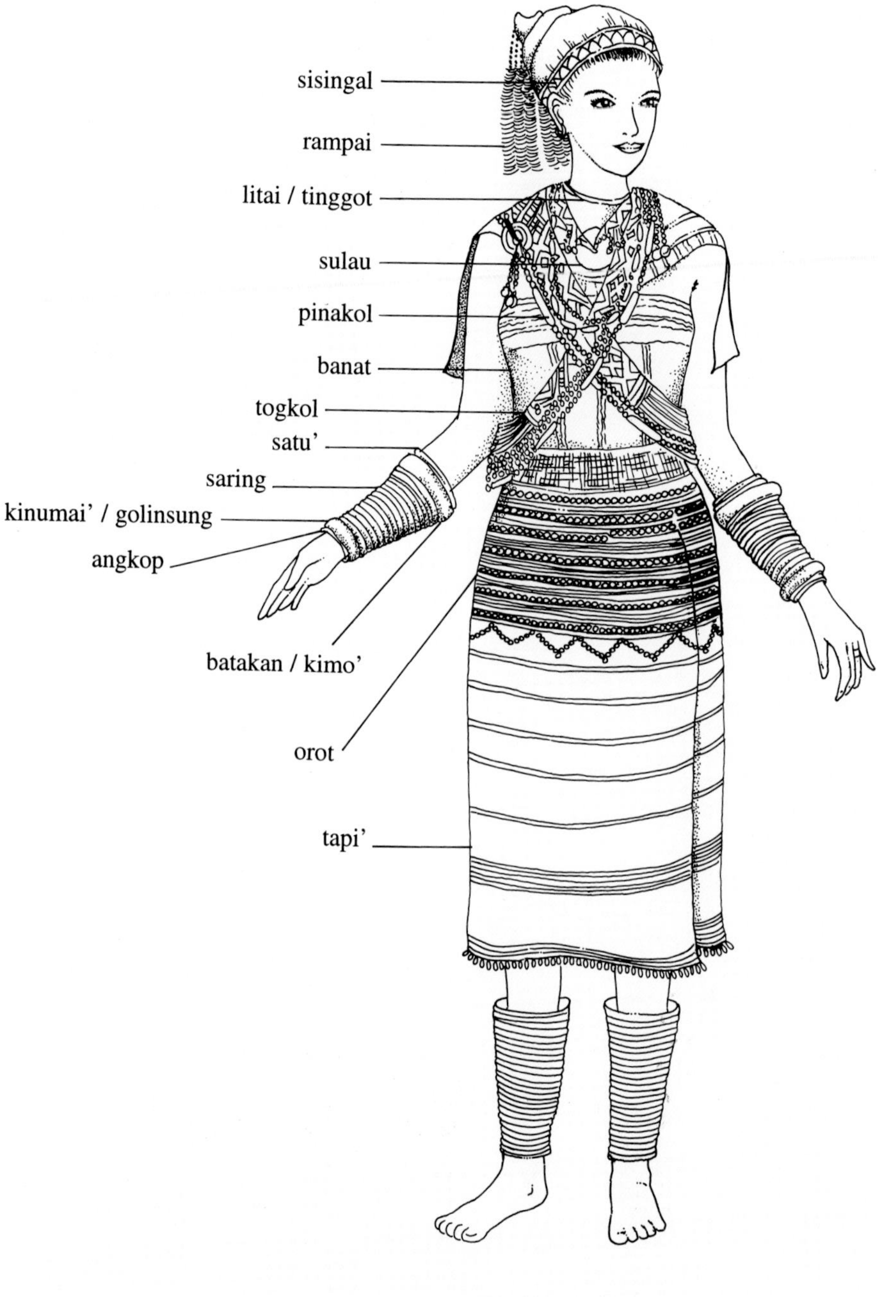

A Rungus lady in traditional costume.

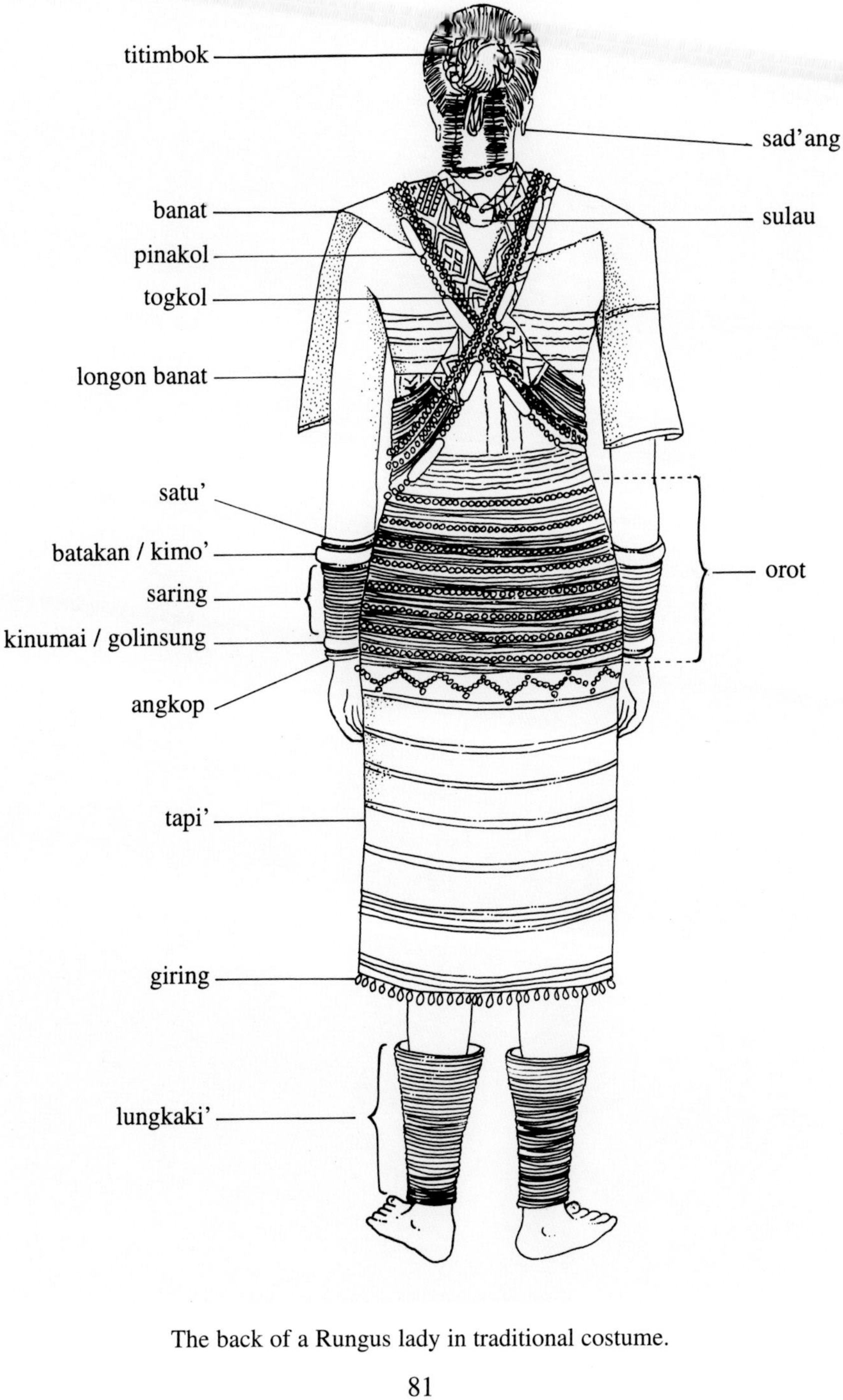

The back of a Rungus lady in traditional costume.

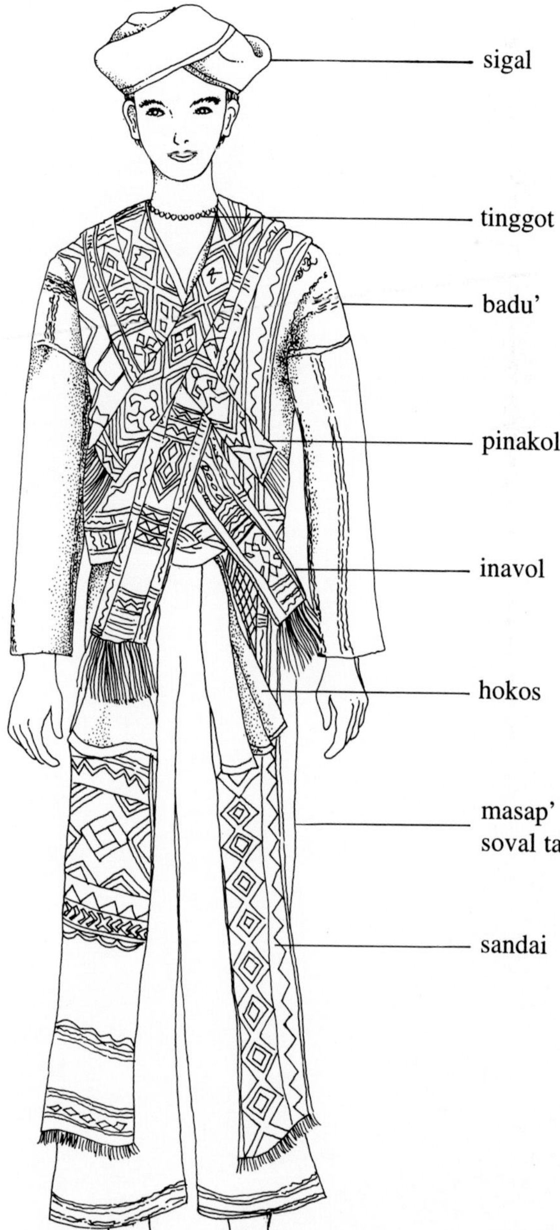

A Rungus man in traditional costume.

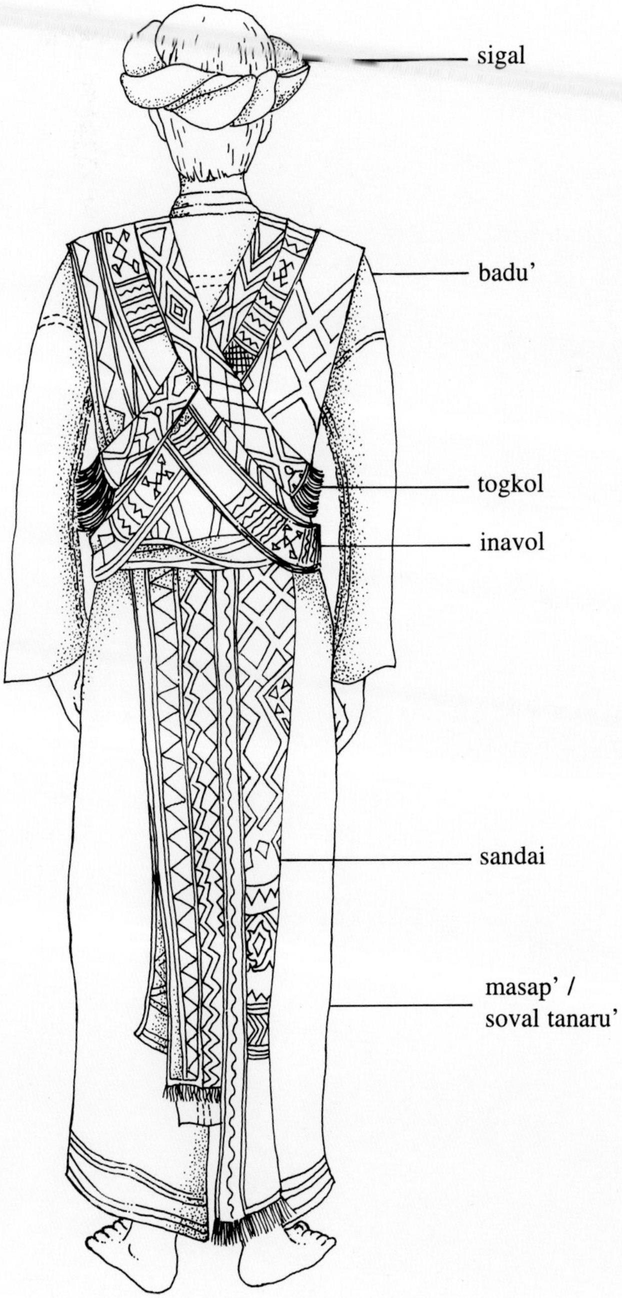

The back of a Rungus man in traditional costume.

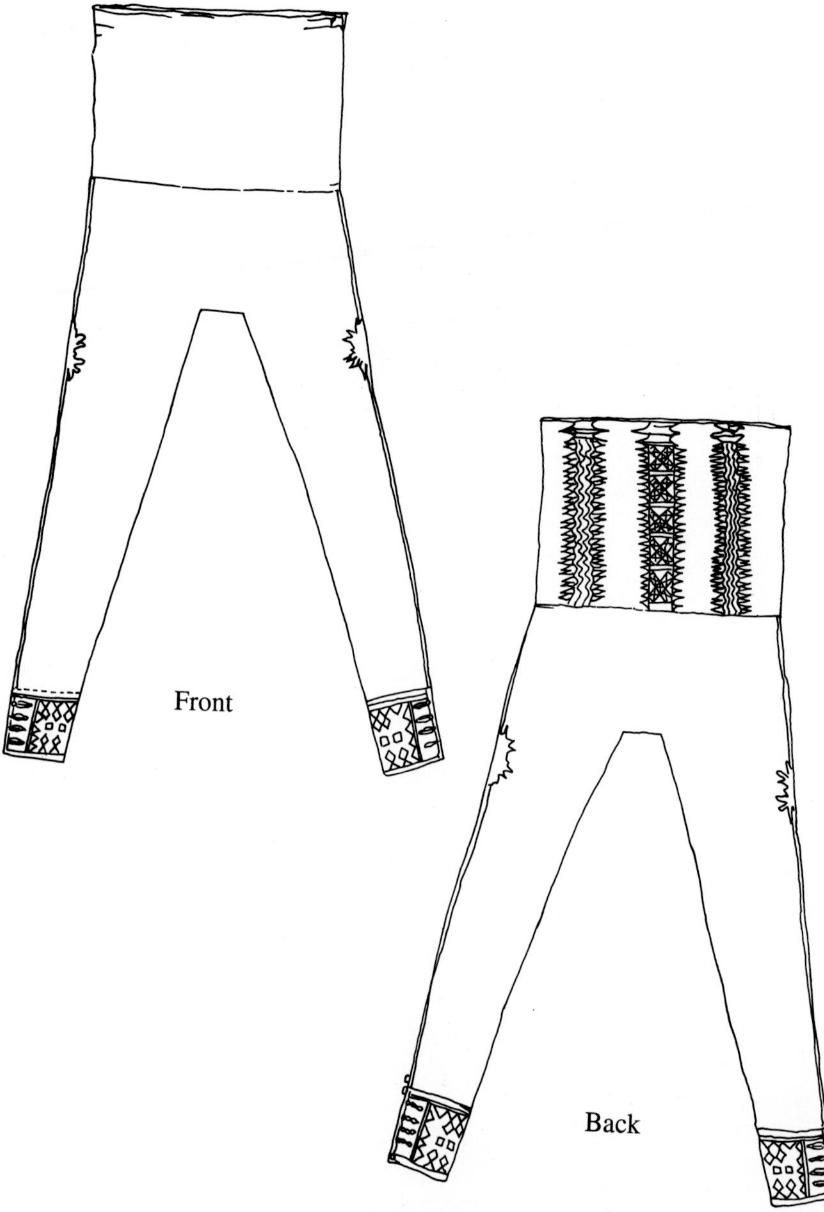

The front and back of a Rungus baggy trousers.

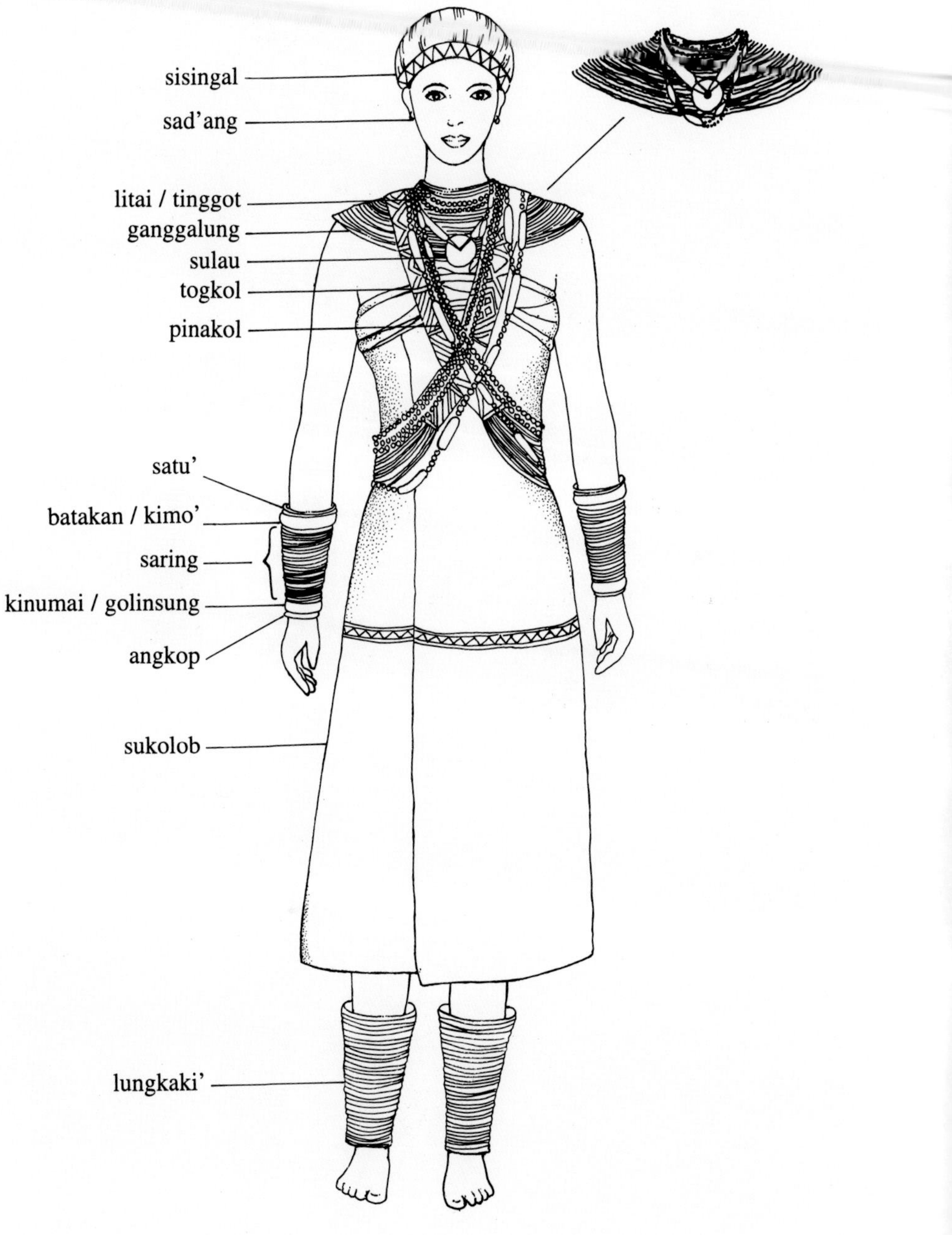

A Rungus lady in her *sukolob.*

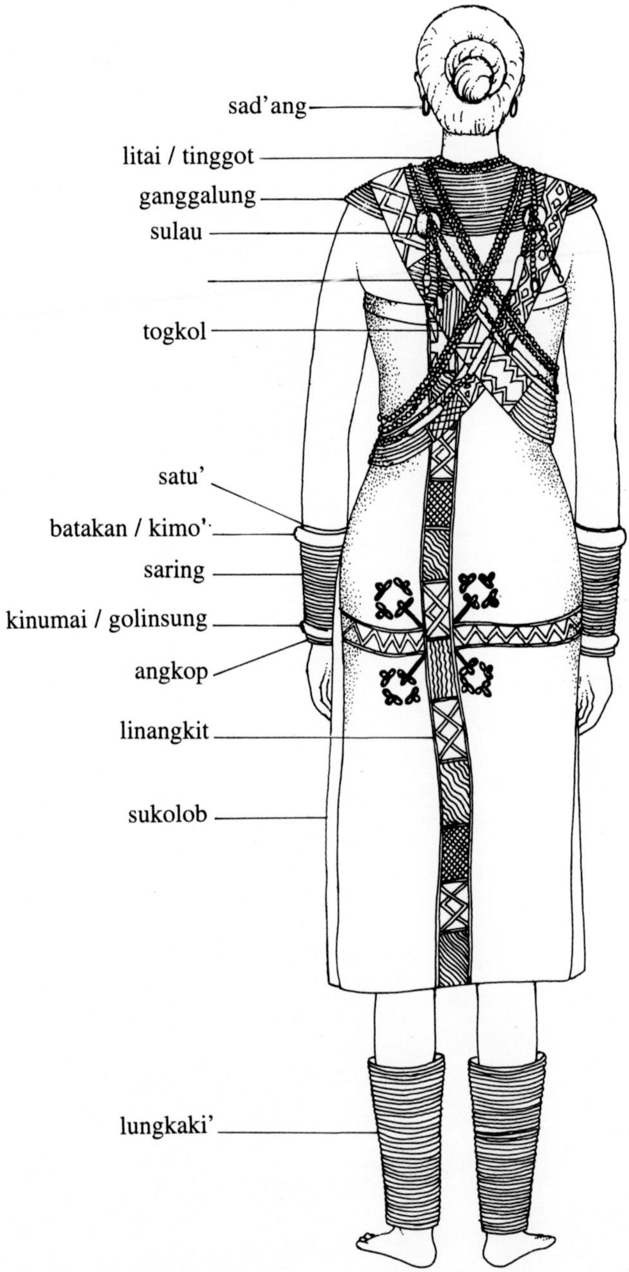

The back of a Rungus lady in her *sukolob*.

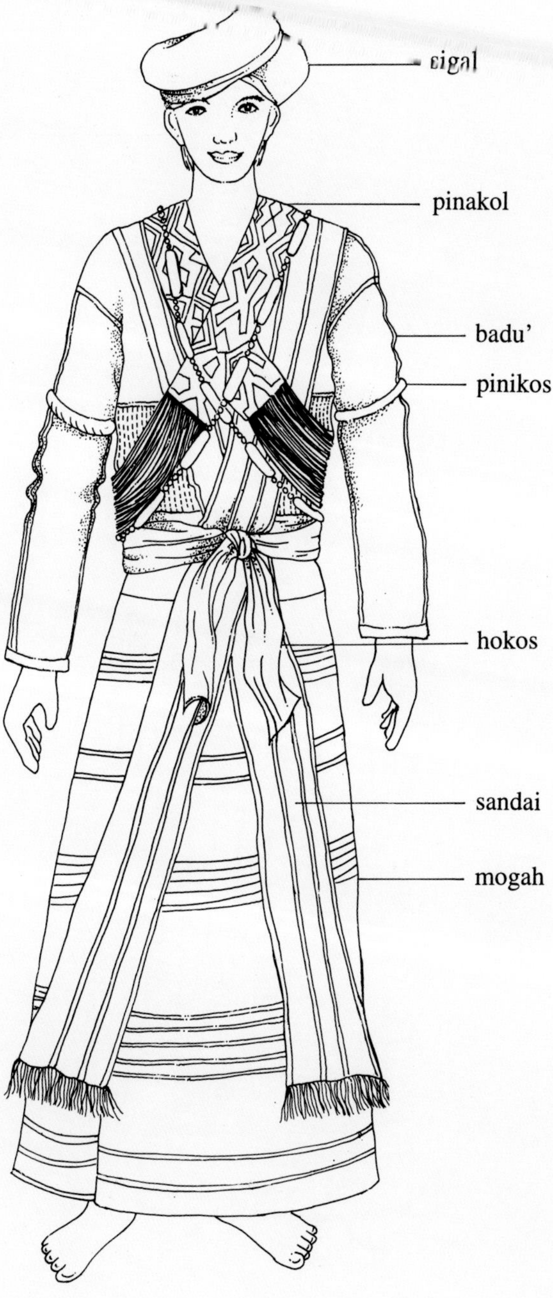

A Rungus man in his *mogah.*

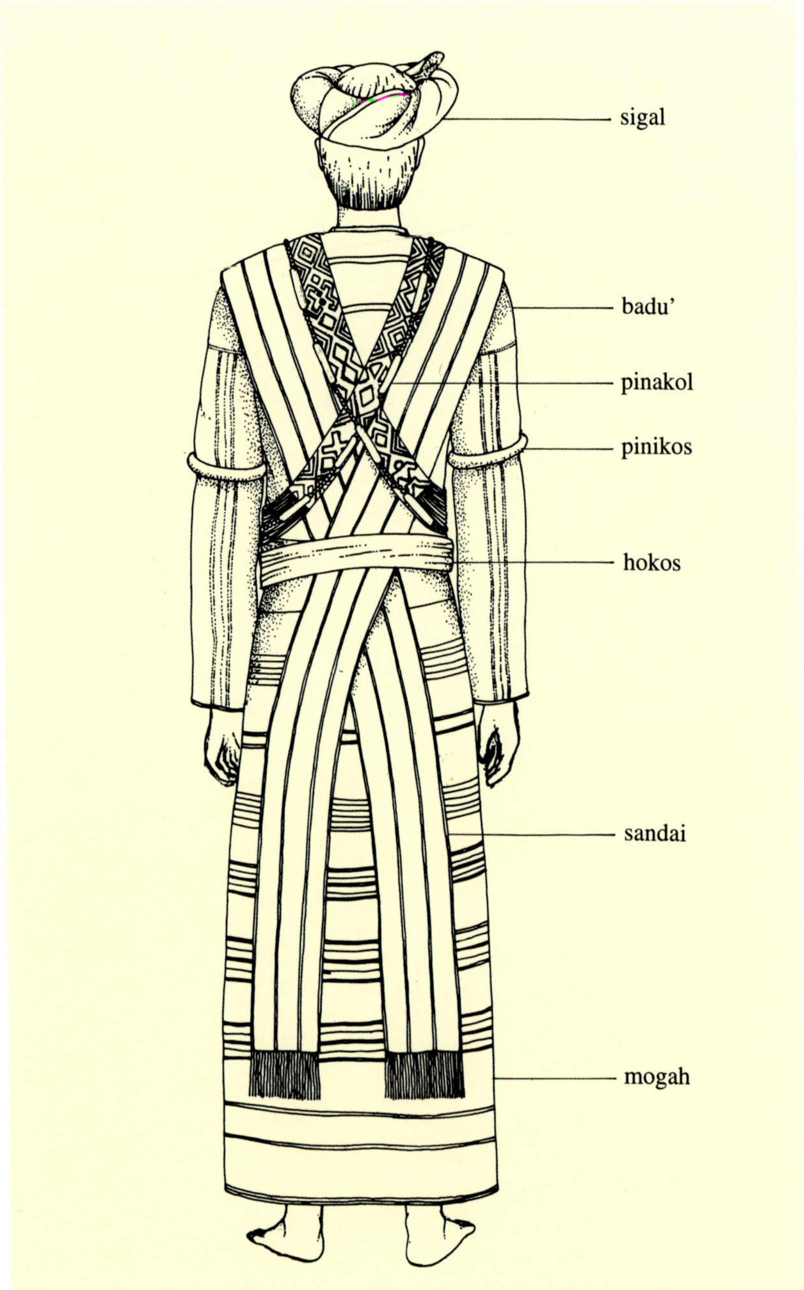

The back of a Rungus man in his *mogah.*

TRADITIONAL COSTUME OF THE RUNGUS

Textile

Basic material: Locally produced, handspun, handwoven cotton: indigo-dyed and decorated with off-white floating weft motifs.

Costume of Women

banat Tight bodice fastened with a button to a rectangular shouldercloth *(longon banat)* with a slit in the middle for the head and loose ends hanging over the shoulders. The narrow upper zone of the bodice *(dokot)* is decorated with horizontal bands filled with floating weft and/or embroidered motifs. These geometric motifs consist of diamonds, triangles, hooks and zig-zags. The lower part of the *banat* is embellished with vertical bands. Centre front is usually a horizontal diabolo with a male and female figure in each triangle and at the sides one or more black lizards on a white field.

tapi' Tube-skirt falling below the knees. [Priestesses wear a *tapi'* with heavy brass bells at the hem to accompany the chants.] The floating weft motifs in the horizontal bands comprise an astonishing range of subjects. There is a fern motif, vegetable seeds, a drunken woman and a pattern derived from the body of the black bird. Worn during festival or ceremonies.

sukolob Calf-length blue or black commercial cotton wrap tied over the chest. One long strip of *linangkit/rinangkit* along the vertical seam is intersected by a horizontal one in the middle of the *sukolob*. On the intersection four floral motifs in needle embroidery radiate from the centre. The pattern of the *linangkit/rinangkit* strips consists of separate motifs. On the intersection the horizontal band almost always shows the motifs of a rice field snake. Worn as daily attire.

Notes: Usually the motifs of the *tapi'* and the *sukolob* indicate the social position of the wearer: *sinombitan* for the upper class and *tinongkupan* for the others.

Accessories:

sisingal Several strings of beads tied together, worn around the head.

titimbok Hairpin of wood or rattan, cloth and beads.

sisik Brass decorative haircomb.

sad'ang Brass earrings.

ganggalung Disc of brass coil of approximately 40 cm in diameter worn as a necklace. These cumbersome ornaments are hardly worn anymore. Only in isolated villages will older women still put them on for ceremonial occasions.

litai or ***tinggot*** Narrow choker-like necklace of beadwork.

sulau Necklace of old beads and a disc of white shell, *kima (Tridachna gigas*— giant clam) in front and back. Bells are attached on either side of the disc in front.

togkol String of carnelian, glass and shell beads looped crossed over the shoulders.

pinakol Two bands of beadwork with geometric and human figures looped crossed over the shoulders.

orot Wide hip girdle/belt of coiled brass wire and rows of beads. Worn during weddings and other ceremonies.

giring Small round brass bells sewn at the hem of the *tapi'*.

lungkaki' Tightly coiled brass ornament covering the lower leg. Just like the *ganggalung* these heavy leggings have gone out of fashion.

rampai A hairpin which has two or three rows of folded pieces of colourful cloth strung together and which float down to the nape.

The following types of bracelets are always worn in the same order. Often the traditional materials have been substituted by plastic but nevertheless these bracelets are felt to be a sign of Rungus identity. These are worn daily and during ceremonies.

satu' Bracelet of coconut shell worn below the elbow.

batakan or ***kimo'*** Bracelet of shell *(kima).*

saring Brass coiled wire bracelet covering most of the underarm. The *saring* is enclosed by the *satu* and *batakan* and *angkop.*

kinumai or ***golinsung*** Bracelet of shell *(kima).*

angkop Bracelet of coconut shell-like *satu'* around the wrist.

Costume of Men

badu'	Long-sleeved handwoven shirt with geometric motifs.
soval sarabulu'	Baggy trousers with wide waistline and *rinangkit* decorated seams. Plain trousers, without *rinangkit* are called *masap* or *souval tanaru'*.
hokos	Waistband of long strips of red, green and yellow cotton, sewn together.
sandai	Two folded lengths of printed commercial fabric falling down from each shoulder to the calves.
inavol	Narrow handwoven circular sashes with geometric motifs worn crosswise over the chest.
sigal	Headdress of folded *pis* cloth produced by Binadan craftswomen.
mogah	*Sarong* made from *mogah* cloth woven by Iranun weavers. Worn during the *mogigol* dance.
pinakol	Two bands of beadwork with geometric and human figures looped crossed over the shoulders.
tinggot	Narrow choker-like necklace of beadwork.
pinikos	Upper arm bracelet made of hardwood.

Sabah Motifs and Special Items

LINANGKIT

Patience and long experience are prerequisites for the creation of a fine piece of *linangkit*. The term *linangkit* here is used generically to refer to a special needle work technique that is practised by the women of many ethnic groups of west and north of Sabah and it is a unique feature of their textiles.

Linangkit closely resembles the European technique of 'tatting' or 'frivolité', a French word used in other languages as well. In English, *linangkit* is sometimes referred to as 'needle weave' or 'tapestry weave'. But these descriptions do not sufficiently illustrate how it is done. Tatting or frivolité is done with a small bobbin and results in a lace-like fabric that is ideal for trimming, and so on.

In Sabah, the *linangkit* is done with a needle: a thin thread is looped into countless interconnecting identical knots. This produces a dense strong fabric.

The Sabahan *linangkit*-tradition is still found done only on the north and west coast. It probably comes from the Kudat area in the north where material culture is strongly influenced by the Philippines.

There, the Maranao and Magindanao of Mindanao Island, in the Philippines, make so-called *langkit* for the same purpose: as a decorative way to join two panels of (handwoven) cloth. These are usually handwoven on the loom.

Some Philippine motifs, however, seem to be older than the Sabahan ones: pre-historic lozenges and hooks are prevalent. These do appear in some Sabahan weaving (Rungus floating weft motifs) but they are curiously absent from the *linangkit* motif inventory.

In most industrialized areas of the world, 'tatting' has become obsolete as so many other time-consuming manual production methods. But here, in the wet-rice cultivating west and north coastal groups, *linangkit* is still admired and widely used, although the age of the female makers is getting more and more advanced.

It takes many months to complete one piece of *linangkit*, with its tiny knots. Moreover, the work is done after household chores, working in the padi-fields and minding the family. Experienced women do not need an example to work from, but they must have good eye-sight or good glasses and sufficient light. They must also concentrate for all the knots must be counted to get the pattern just right.

Photo: Sabah Museum

Lotud *Linangkit.*

WHO ARE THE WOMEN WHO STILL MAKE *LINANGKIT*?

Dusun Kwijau

The Dusun Kwijau in Keningau, in the interior of Sabah, apply narrow strips of *linangkit* along the side seams of their ceremonial blouses.

Papar Kadazan

In the Papar region, the Kadazan women traditionally decorate their black skirts with a band of *linangkit*, though these days it has been replaced with a panel of cross-stitch which are easier to make. The Penampang Kadazan rarely apply it: their preference for unobtrusive embroidery may account for this restraint.

Lotud

In the black ceremonial costumes of the Lotud, however, *linangkit* is a striking feature. Circular sashes, knee-length skirts and the back below the waistband of men's trousers (*binandus*) are all embellished with this type of needlework. The wide continuous band displays a repeating pattern with crosses—inspired by melon seeds—in the middle. These are usually surrounded by squares, built up of opposing triangles in contrasting colours. The squares are said to be a stylized beetle. Formerly, the curved iridescent hard wings of these same beetles were used to make the strings dangling from the *siwot* (head decoration).

For the Lotud women, the colour-arrangement within the geometric motifs is a matter of personal taste, but just as elsewhere they stick to local traditions where the range of colours is concerned. Orange and red are dominant here, with purple, green, yellow and black and white for smaller areas. Nowadays, the yarn is always bought in a local shop.

Bajau

A wide band of *linangkit* in the front of a long black matrimonial skirt used to be a tradition of the Bajau as well. For their wedding celebrations the Bajau prefer motifs which represent the natural world and therefore new life.

Called *berangkit* by the Bajau, the *linangkit* on the bridal costume displays big stylized cotton flower *(bunga kapas)* and the bamboo shoot *(pucuk rebung).*

In general, the *linangkit*-maker is not strictly bound in the arrangement of patterns. The symbolic significance of the motifs is not always known to her and it does not seem to be a decisive factor. Motifs from other ethnic groups are frequently borrowed: such as motifs from the Bajau *kain dastar*.

Dusun Tindal

The Dusun Tindal in the area of Tempasuk like to have *linangkit* on their wedding costumes: men and women wear identical black blouses with *linangkit* running over the sleeves from the shoulders till the elbow where it is slit open. Their sleeveless blouses have *linangkit* along the seams.

Rungus

In the Rungus version of *linangkit*, which they call *rangkit*, the geometric motifs are usually separated from one another in defined boxes or compartments. The Rungus women seem to favour a balance between warm and cool hues without a strongly dominant colour.

The origin of most Rungus motifs is fairly easy to trace as they are taken from daily life and their environment such as butterflies, pythons, leaves, stars, shells, stairs and the pattern of dog feet.

The *pinakol* motif of two diagonal lines represents the two sashes worn over the chest by the men at ceremonial occasions.

Linangkit also forms part of the Rungus costume of men *(sarabulu),* sewn below the waistband on the back of trousers like the costume for Lotud men. It is fitted in two long strips into the *sukolob*, the calf-length blue *sarong* which is the daily outfit of Rungus women, and is tied above the breast.

One strip runs horizontal and the other encircles the hips. Where they intersect, there is almost always a zig-zag ricefield-snake motif in the wider band going downwards. In the corners, four radiating floral patterns are embroidered in a flat satin stitch.

KAIN PIS

Kain Pis is a one-metre square of two facing pieces of cloth richly embroidered with colourful stylised motifs. It is reversible. The completed piece is usually folded, tied and worn as a headgear mostly by Rungus men. The men of other ethnic groups of Sabah also wear it.

Legend of *Kain Pis*

The origin of the *Kain Pis* is associated with the Suluk community who were seafarers originating from the Sulu Archipelago of the Philippines. Therefore, the motifs found in the *kain pis* have been profoundly influenced by their lifestyle. The motifs embroidered on the *kain pis* such as *kaliagah* (similar to a dragon), spider, fish and bird (*Agira*) contained legends. The most prominent theme is the *kaliagah.*

Photo: Sabah Museum

(Left) A *Kain Pis.*

According to the Suluk people, the *kaliagah* is a kind of animal, which although it resembles a fierce dragon, it inspires beauty.

According to the legend, while going about their daily chores by the river one day, some women saw a beautiful vision of a fairy-like water creature with its long body swaying to the rhythm of the water. They were so enthralled by the scene that they desired to get close to it. But alas, they then realised that what they were seeing was only an image created by the sun rays hitting the water surface. As a result of this experience, the women tried to capture the beauty of the water creature—the *kaliagah*, into their embroidery—the *kain pis*.

The spider motif is said to be associated with the Prophet Muhammad. According to the story, one day, the Prophet while eluding his enemies who were out to kill him, sheltered inside a cave. As soon as he was inside the cave, the spider quickly spun its web across the entrance of the cave. The enemies who were pursuing the Prophet, on seeing the undisturbed cobweb went past the entrance. The swift and clever action of the spider thus endeared the creature to the Prophet, and thus, the spider is regarded with respect.

The motif of the bird, *Agira*, is a mythical double-headed bird which guards the corner of the *kain pis*. It is believed to be a foreteller of good or bad news and is regarded as a guardian by the Suluk people. From a vantage point up on a roof or tree, it is able to tell the advance of friends or foes and sounds off the appropriate warning.

A spider motif woven in the *Kain Pis*.

Other motifs which form the background of the *kain pis* such as butterflies, flowers (*Kembang Tuleh*, a legume—*Sesbania grandiflora*) and foliage (*Kembang Janggayan*) are also included because they are the playmate or associated with the *kaliagah*.

A complēted *kain pis* depicts the worldview of the Suluk people and their kindred groups such as the Binadan. This legend of the *kain pis* and the technique of embroidery are handed down from generation to generation.

Embroidery

Two facing pieces of plain cotton cloths of contrasting colours, measuring 1.4 metre square each are placed on a square frame. The cloths are pulled at the sides and tied by strings to the frame to ensure an even tension. The cloths are usually of black and red, or black and orange, or orange and red, or orange and yellow.

Traditionally, the desired motifs are drawn on paper first. The outline of the drawings is then perforated with tiny holes. The paper is then placed on the cloth and fine grey powder (made from crushed incinerated shell) is sprinkled on it. By gently tapping the paper, the fine powder is filtered through the holes. The paper is then removed, leaving the outline—the "guided print" of the drawing on the surface of the cloth.

The patterns are "drawn" beginning from the corners and the sides and then moving inwards in order to keep the drawings well balanced between all four corners of the cloth.

When the whole surface is thus "drawn", the cloth is ready to be embroidered. The embroidery follows this pattern, working from the sides inwards. It is sewn in such as way that the pattern mirror the other side, so that both sides can be used. The knots and ends are discreetly hidden.

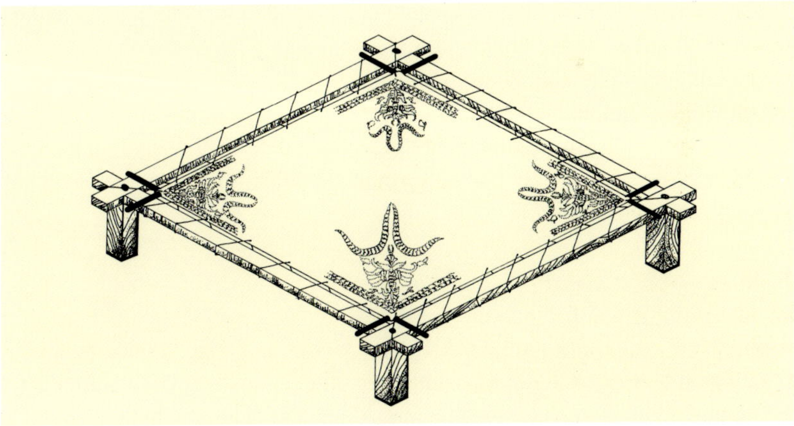

Square-frame for *Kain Pis* embroidery.

Nowadays, the patterns are drawn using carbon paper or drawn free-hand with a pencil.

Bright coloured cotton threads are used for the embroidery, normally no less than seven colours. The main stitch used is the satin stitch which is a versatile filling stitch. On the cloth, it is used for outlines or small shapes, with the stitches running vertically, horizontally or diagonally, to create a dense texture.

A completed *kain pis* may take some three months to finish. The *kain pis* in the Sabah Museum are made by the Binadan, a tribe of the Sulu and Bajau peoples, living near Kudat.

KAIN DASTAR

Traditional weaving

The body-tension or backstrap loom with the continuous warp is the implement most widely used by different ethnic groups to weave traditional cloth. The looms are not large and can be rolled up, carried, easily set up and generally require only a small space to work. The weaver sits on the ground or low stool before the loom with an attachment around her waist or hip and the warp beam secured to a support in front. She braces her feet against the support and uses her body to keep the warp threads taut.

Cloth woven on these looms are generally not very large, corresponding in size to the width of the loom and length of the warp threads. To make larger lengths of cloth, two or more pieces of separately woven cloth are usually joined together.

*Kain dastar**

The Bajau and Iranun of Kota Belud weave a metre-square piece of traditional cloth called *kain dastar*. This piece of cloth when folded and

*The terms used to describe the different parts of the loom are Iranun words.

Photo: Sabah Museum

(Above) A *Kain Dastar* from Kota Belud

Photo: Sabah Museum

(Left) *Siga*—a folded *Kain Dastar*.

tied to make the headcloth or *sigah* is worn by almost every indigenous group in Sabah.

In weaving the *kain dastar*, the warp threads are spread evenly over the warp beam (*saulaya'*) and the breast beam (*taru'an*). The warp beam is tied to a supporting horizontal beam (*paguta'*) while the breast beam is tied to the back strap (*dapi*). A bamboo rod (*liliden*) helps to keep the warp threads straight in their place during weaving.

The shed stick (*bibitan sa pakan*) is used to count and separate the even from the odd threads of the warp yarn. Another shed stick (*bibitan sa aran*) is used for patterns and motifs. A heddle (*bubungen*) is inserted between the even and odd threads, then raised and a wooden shuttle (*tulak*) with the weft inside it is passed through. The counting and separating of the warp threads is repeated and the shuttle sent to the opposite direction. The loosely woven portion is made tight by beating-in the weft with a heavy slightly tapered wooden bar (*barira*).

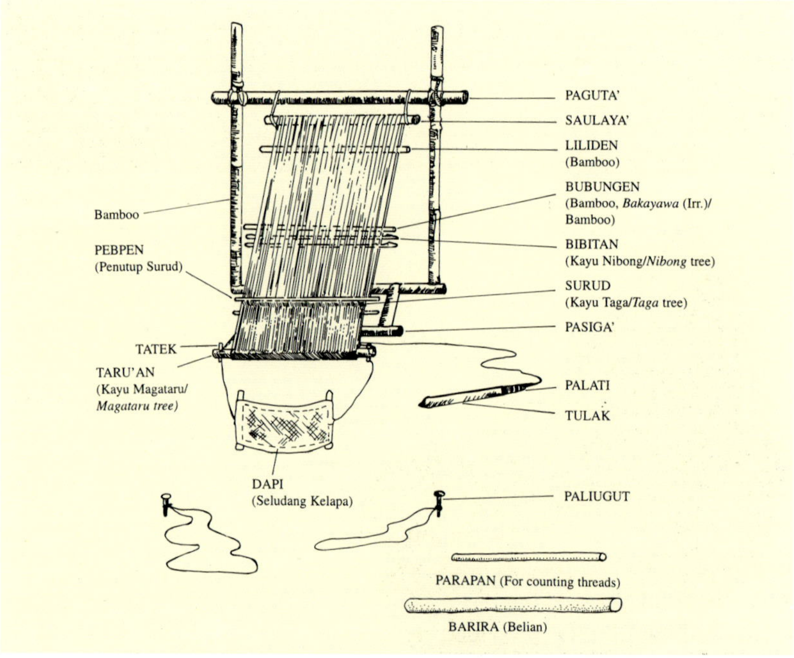

An Iranun backstrap loom.

Acknowledgements

Many people have supported the research for this book. Ms Madelon Boeye from the Netherlands coordinated the research with Sabah Museum staff. A number of village elders have volunteered information, corrected errors and clarified myths, which were essential to the publication of accurate descriptions. Ms Caroline Wiedenhof, Second Secretary of the Royal Netherlands Embassy in Kuala Lumpur, and Dr Corry Klugkist of NUFFIC (Netherlands University Foundation for International Cooperation), the Netherlands are among those who made the research for this publication possible.

For providing information for this book, we would like to record our appreciation to the following persons:—
Puan Cenderamata Sinteh from Kota Belud for providing information on the Bajau traditional costumes; Encik Sarintim Kudandan of Kampung Tampasuk Satu, Kota Belud for giving information on the traditional costumes of the Dusun Tindal of Kota Belud; Puan Anita Nandu from Kampung Diau, Papar for giving information about the Papar Kadazan traditional costumes; Puan Catherine Agang from Kampung Tuavon, Penampang and Puan Rosina Sogondu from Kampung Nampasan, Penampang, for giving information on the Penampang Kadazan traditional costumes; Puan Uwoi bte. Bialah of Kampung Panjut, Tuaran for giving information on the Lotud traditional costumes; Encik Jomihot Sasam of Kampung Tinangol, Kudat for giving information on the Rungus traditional costumes and Puan Unsot bte. Ansulong of Kampung Takilis, Pensiangan for giving information on the Murut traditional costumes.

We also wish to thank Encik Rebbin Noyo and Encik Ismail Mansor for their assistance. Special thanks also to C.L. Chan, David Lee and Benedict Topin for permission to use their fine photographs. We are also grateful for assistance provided by Jacqueline Chu, Jacky Chua Kok Hian and Connie Wong during the final stages of publication.

Bibliography

Benggon Charuruks, Irene and Janette Padasian (eds.) 1992. *Cultures, Customs and Traditions of Sabah, Malaysia: An Introduction.* Sabah Tourism Promotion Corporation, Kota Kinabalu, Sabah. iv + 104 pp.

Blood, Doris E. 1993. Planting and Harvesting. *Sabah Museum Journal* 1(1): 31–37.

Lingenfelter, Sherwood G. (ed.) 1990. *Social Organization of Sabah Societies.* Department of Sabah Museum and State Archives, Kota Kinabalu, Sabah.

Pang, Ngan Yue. 1989. *Tales of the Suluk headgear.* Berita Shell, July 1989, pp. 10–13.

Porodong, Paul. 1992. SIGAH: KAJIAN SATU ASPEK KEBUDAYAAN KEBENDAAN DI SABAH. [Sigah: A study on one aspect of material culture in Sabah.] Latihan Ilmiah bagi memenuhi sebahagian daripada syarat-syarat untuk Ijazah Sarjana Muda Sains, Universiti Malaya, Kuala Lumpur. (Unpublished B.A. thesis.)

Sabah Times. 1990. *"Tengkolok Suluk dengan 'cerita berkaitannya'".* 19 August, 1990.

Sabah Museum. 1991. Traditional Weaving and Dyeing Workshop. Department of Sabah Museum and State Archives, Kota Kinabalu, Sabah.

Sabah Museum. 1992. *Sabah's Heritage: A Brief Introduction to Sabah's History and Heritage.* Department of Sabah Museum, Kota Kinabalu, Sabah.

Index

C

D

E

F

G

H

N

O

P

R

S

T

U

V

W

Y